ANCIENT CHRISTIAN WRITERS

THE WORKS OF THE FATHERS IN TRANSLATION

EDITED BY

JOHANNES QUASTEN, S. T. D.
*Professor of Ancient Church History
and Christian Archaeology*

JOSEPH C. PLUMPE, PH. D.
*Professor of Patristic Greek
and Ecclesiastical Latin*

The Catholic University of America
Washington, D. C.

No. 3

WESTMINSTER, MARYLAND

THE NEWMAN PRESS

LONDON

LONGMANS, GREEN AND CO.

ST. AUGUSTINE

FAITH
HOPE AND CHARITY

ENCHIRIDION

DE FIDE SPE ET CARITATE

ST. AUGUSTINE

FAITH
HOPE AND CHARITY

TRANSLATED AND ANNOTATED

BY

THE VERY REVEREND
LOUIS A. ARAND, S. S., S. T. D.

President of Divinity College
Catholic University of America
Washington, D. C.

WESTMINSTER, MARYLAND

THE NEWMAN PRESS

LONDON

LONGMANS, GREEN AND CO.

THE NEWMAN PRESS

WESTMINSTER MD USA

LONGMANS, GREEN AND CO LTD

6 & 7 CLIFFORD STREET LONDON W I

BOSTON HOUSE STRAND STREET CAPE TOWN

531 LITTLE COLLINS STREET MELBOURNE

ORIENT LONGMANS LTD

BOMBAY CALCUTTA MADRAS

Second Printing
Third Printing 1955

CONTENTS

ST. AUGUSTINE

FAITH
HOPE AND CHARITY

Augustine, *Retractationes* 2. 63: I have also written a book on Faith, Hope, and Charity. The occasion was a request by the person to whom it is addressed that I write for him a little volume which he could always have at hand, a book of the sort called *enchiridion* by the Greeks. In this work I have, I think, given a sufficiently thorough survey of the worship which we must give to God. That this constitutes true wisdom in man, is established by Divine Scripture. The book begins as follows: "I cannot tell you, beloved Laurentius, how delighted I am with your learning."

INTRODUCTION

The title given to the book here offered in a new translation is the only one by which the author himself referred to it. For centuries past it has been more familiarly known as the *Enchiridion*, due no doubt to the fact that three times in the treatise itself (4, 6, 122) mention is made by St. Augustine of the request he had received from a certain Laurentius to compose for him an *enchiridion*,[1] or handbook, which would touch briefly on the principal points of the Christian faith. Augustine took some pains to show that he himself had so understood the request and then set himself to the task. Although he allowed himself at times to be drawn into rather lengthy discussions, he nevertheless always remained aware of his main purpose. Even so, when he reached the end of the treatise he had composed, he expressed his doubts as to whether he had really succeeded in holding the finished product down to an *enchiridion* such as Laurentius had requested, and preferred him to be the judge.[2]

But the term *Enchiridion* can only indicate the purpose of an author to present something in outline; it tells us nothing about the contents of the book or the nature of the thing outlined. Hence, it has seemed preferable to give to the treatise the title by which Augustine himself always referred to it, lifting it from the position of sub-title to which custom has relegated it. In his *Retractationes* (2. 63), for instance, he tells us very simply that he had written " a book on *Faith, Hope, and Charity*." Now, since this is precisely what he did, we beg to present this little volume as St. Augustine's treatise on *Faith, Hope, and Charity*.[3]

In the introduction to this work (3) the Bishop of Hippo expresses his conviction that all those things which are to be known and sought after in religion center about the objects of faith, hope, and charity. Then, a little later, he tells Laurentius that these objects are summed up in the Lord's Prayer and the Creed (7). Here was the announcement of the plan he intended to follow in placing in the hands of his spiritual son Laurentius a manual of Christian doctrine.

The idea was not original with St. Augustine, for by his time both the Creed and the Lord's Prayer had become traditional media for imparting explanations of the Church's principal teachings. However, it seems beyond question that in the hands of Augustine they became a much more highly efficient instrument than they had been for his predecessors. This is especially true of the Creed, which he used also in other works [4] as a framework within which to sketch the Christian beliefs in outline. In fact, there are those [5] who are convinced that it is due precisely to Augustine's extraordinary success in the use he made of it that the Creed remained in the West a leavening influence in religious life and teaching, and that centuries later St. Thomas Aquinas, the greatest mind in the history of Christian thought since Augustine himself, could find no better model for his *Compendium theologiae* than this treatise built on the Apostles' Creed.[6]

To a man proposing to himself to use the Creed today as a vehicle of religious instruction, Augustine's presentation may well seem remarkable both for what it includes and what it omits. Whether or not one agrees that all the topics introduced into the book by Augustine find their place naturally within the framework of the Creed,[7] one cannot but marvel at the wide range of topics and the mental acumen with which the great bishop discusses them. This strikes one all the more forcibly when one recalls that Augustine was consciously striving to keep his presentation within the proper limits of an outline or manual. While it is true that the book was written in the later days of his episcopacy, when many of the great controversial issues were quite dead, it nevertheless contains echoes of practically all of them. How else explain his long excursion into the problem of evil, if it be not for the memory of his battles with the Manichaeans; or that lengthy discussion of the morality of error and lying, except for the experience he had had with the Academics; or the tremendous insistence in practically every page of the treatise on the absolutely gratuitous character of God's grace, if it be not because of his long-drawn-out struggle with that most formidable enemy, an enemy that was still harassing him, Pelagianism? That he should have touched on all these problems even in a compendium of Christian doctrine is completely understandable; but that he should have allowed himself to treat them in such minute detail is difficult to explain unless the reason be those titanic struggles which he had waged, first in search of truth, and then to preserve and defend it.

If the inclusion, therefore, of some details of doctrine tends on first sight to give occasion for surprise, may one not, without being accused of casting aspersions on one of the greatest names in Christian history, also express some little wonderment over the omission, partial or total, of certain ideas which today we should desire to find even in a summary of Christian doctrine? One thinks, for instance, of the Holy Sacrifice of the Mass, though he does make mention of it late in the book (110); or of the great doctrine of

Redemption through the God-Man, to which he gives relatively so little space, or of the Church and its hierarchy and its liturgy. Moreover, since he set out to write a treatise on faith, hope, and charity, one looks, but in vain, for a discussion of charity more or less commensurate with that on faith. If these lacunae give rise to a sense of regret, the disappointment comes not so much from a conviction of failure on the part of St. Augustine, but rather from the realization of how much he could have enlightened and edified us had he elected to discuss these points of doctrine with something of the thoroughness with which he treats, for example, the problem of evil.

But while this lack of proportion may seem to us today to constitute a defect, it was not necessarily so in the time when the book was written. Nor does it in any way detract from the larger fact that St. Augustine has given us in this little volume a fairly complete compendium of his whole theology and the system on which it rests. Had we only this one work of his, we should be able to form a rather adequate estimate of his place in theology. So true is this that when A. Harnack came to conclude his long dissertation on Augustine's place in the history of dogma, he found no better way than to give a summarized exposition of the Christian doctrines which Augustine has expressed in the present treatise.[8]

In *Faith, Hope, and Charity* St. Augustine begins practically with the doctrine of creation, with man in a state of supernatural and therefore wholly unmerited perfection. He then dwells on the fall of our first parents, which reduced mankind to a *massa damnationis* and made all men subject to the eternal punishment of hell. He goes on to demonstrate that just as our creation was a free gift from God, so our deliverance from that *massa damnationis* through the In-

carnation and sacrificial death of the God-Man likewise was
due solely to the utterly gratuitous mercy of the Godhead.
To make and preserve us members of the Mystical Body of
Christ, he tells us, we have the Church, the sacraments, the
Sacrifice of the Altar, prayer, and almsgiving. From first to
last he stresses the love and mercy of God and the absolute
freedom with which He bestows the gifts whereby the elect
attain heaven through unmerited mercy. In all God's deal-
ings with men St. Augustine is absolutely certain of two
things: it is God's grace freely given which saves man; and
under grace man freely works out his own salvation. He sees
the profound mystery this involves, but he chooses to leave
it where St. Paul had left it before him, in the inscrutable
mind of God.[9] The entire book is, therefore, as Paul Simon
so aptly puts it,[10] a song of praise to honor the grace of God,
and could be epitomized in the memorable lines of the
Imitation of Christ: " In this, Lord, thou hast most showed
the sweetness of thy charity to me, that when I was not, thou
madest me; and when I wandered far from thee thou
broughtest me again to serve thee, and commandeth me to
love thee." [11]

Our treatise was written not earlier than the end of the
year 420 and not later than 423. In it Augustine makes
mention of his work *Contra mendacium* (18), which was
very probably published in the year 420. He further refers
to an event which is clearly dated—the death of his great
contemporary, St. Jerome (87), who died on September 30th,
420. Now, since Augustine speaks of the present work in
his *De octo Dulcitii quaestionibus* (1. 10), which critics
agree appeared about 422-23, his *Enchiridion* must be placed
between the end of the year 420 as the *terminus a quo* and
the year 423 as the *terminus ad quem*. The Benedictines of

St. Maur also point out [12] that in the *Retractationes* the work follows the *Contra Iulianum*, published about the year 421. They seem to think that the *Enchiridion* should be assigned to the same year, and this opinion has been accepted quite generally ever since.

It is quite impossible to establish with any certainty the identity of the addressee, Laurentius, to whose request for religious instruction the world owes the treatise. In some later manuscripts he is termed a high official—*primicerius, primicerius notariorum urbis Romae, primicerius urbis Romanae*—and in one of them he is given the rank of deacon. However, this information appears to have been derived from the fact that in the *De octo Dulcitii quaestionibus* (1. 10) Laurentius is termed a brother of Dulcitius, and the further fact that we are told in the *Retractationes* (2. 59) that Dulcitius had been sent by the emperor Honorius as an emissary to Africa to supervise the enforcement of the anti-Donatist legislation. At any rate, the conclusion that Laurentius and Dulcitius belonged to a family of some distinction seems justified. Add to this the fact that St. Augustine commends Laurentius for his learning and studiousness (1, 122). Dulcitius, it appears, was on his African assignment in the year 420. It is of course possible that Laurentius accompanied or joined him there and that both became acquainted with the venerable Bishop of Hippo.[13] That Augustine calls Laurentius his son and in his closing lines tells him of his special affection for him, might be taken to indicate a relation of close friendship. But this can lead only to a measure of probability. The courtesies of formal epistolary amenities could very well account for these terms of endearment.

*   *   *

The text used for the present translation is that of J. G. Krabinger (Tübingen 1861) as reproduced, with some few changes, by O. Scheel: *Augustins Enchiridion* (Sammlung ausgewählter kirchen- und dogmengeschichtlicher Quellenschriften, 2. Reihe, Heft 4: 2nd ed., Tübingen 1930). Fortunately, the transmission of the original text through the centuries seems to have been very good.

Other modern versions, to which the translator has sometimes referred, are the following:

Cornish, C. L., in *Seventeen Short Treatises of S. Augustine* (A Library of Fathers of the Holy Catholic Church 22, Oxford 1847) 85-158.

Mitterer, S., in *Des heiligen Kirchenvaters Aurelius Augustinus ausgewählte praktische Schriften, homiletischen und katechetischen Inhalts* (Bibliothek der Kirchenväter 49, Munich 1925) 387-502.

Raulx, M., in *Oeuvres complètes de Saint Augustin* 12 (sous la direction de M. Raulx, Bar-le-Duc 1868) 1-43.

Shaw, J. F., in *St. Augustine: On the Holy Trinity, Doctrinal Treatises, Moral Treatises* (A Select Library of the Nicene and Post-Nicene Fathers of the Christian Church, First Series 3, New York 1905) 229-76.

Simon, P., *Das Handbüchlein des hl. Augustinus* (Dokumente der Religion 1, Paderborn 1923).

CHAPTER 1

St. Augustine consents to write a handbook of Christian doctrine for Laurentius and outlines its nature and contents.

I cannot tell you, beloved son Laurentius, how delighted I am with your learning,[1] and how much I desire that you should be a wise man. Not that you should be one of those of whom it is said: *Where is the wise? Where is the scribe? Where is the disputer of this world? Hath God not made foolish the wisdom of this world?*[2] No, rather should you be of those of whom it is written: *The multitude of the wise is the welfare of the whole world;*[3] and such as the Apostle wishes those to become to whom he says: *But I would have you to be wise in good and simple in evil.*[4] [For, just as no one can exist of himself, so neither can anyone be wise of himself, but needs to be enlightened by Him of whom it is written: *All wisdom is from God.*]

2. For man true wisdom consists in piety. This you will find in the book of the saintly Job, for there you can read what Wisdom herself spoke to man: *Behold, piety is wisdom.*[5] But if you should ask what kind of piety she spoke of in that passage, you will find it termed more accurately in the Greek, *theosébeia*, which means "worship of God." You see, in Greek, piety is also called *eusébeia*, which means "correct worship," although this too refers principally to the worship of God. But there is no more appropriate word than the former, one that plainly gave expression to divine worship when the meaning of human wisdom was formulated.

You are asking me to speak briefly on an important subject: you do not expect me to do this in still fewer words, do
you? Or is it this that you want, that I should give you such
a brief outline and set forth in a short treatise how God
should be worshipped?

3. If I should answer that God is to be worshipped by
faith, hope, and charity, you will doubtless say that the
answer is all too concise for your wishes, and will then beg
for a brief explanation of what each of these three means:
that is, what we must believe, what we must hope for, and
what we must love. If I do this, you will have an answer
to all the questions which you have set down in your letter.
If you have retained a copy of it, it will be easy for you to
return to these matters and to read them over again; if not,
you should recall them as I make mention of them.

4. According to your letter, you wish me to write a book,
to serve you as a handbook, as they call it, something that
would be always within reach. It should contain the answers
to questions such as these: What is most to be sought after?
In view of the various heresies, what is chiefly to be avoided?
To what extent does reason come to the aid of religion, or
to what extent does matter known through faith alone not
fall under the scope of reason? What is the beginning and
what the end of human endeavor? What is the sum total
of all teaching? What is the sure and true foundation of
Catholic faith?

All these things which you ask about you will undoubtedly
know if you understand well what man should believe and
hope for and love. For these are the things which must be
chiefly, nay solely, sought after in religion. He who would
deny them is either a total stranger to the name of Christ,

or he is a heretic. The things which originate in the senses or are discovered by the mind's faculty of understanding, are to be defended by reason. Those things, however, which transcend our sense experience or which we have not grasped and cannot grasp by our own intellect, we must indubitably believe on the testimony of those witnesses by whom the Scriptures,[6] rightfully called divine, were written—witnesses who by divine assistance were enabled either by means of the senses or the mind to see or even to foresee these things.

5. Now, once the mind has been endowed with the beginning of faith *which works through love*,[7] it tends through right living to attain to sight[8] where dwells for the holy and perfect of heart that ineffable beauty, the full vision of which constitutes supreme happiness. Surely, this is the answer to your question: What is the beginning and what the end of human endeavor? We begin in faith and are made perfect by sight. This is at the same time the sum total of all teaching: and the sure and true foundation of Catholic faith is Christ. *For other foundation*, says the Apostle, *no man can lay, but that which is laid, which is Christ Jesus*.[9] Nor is it to be denied that this is the proper foundation of Catholic faith, because it can be held that this is doctrine common to ourselves and to some heretics. For, if we ponder well over the things which pertain to Christ, we shall find that among some heretics who like to be called Christians, Christ is honored in name, though in reality He is not with them.[10] To prove this would take too long, for we should have to mention all the heresies which once were, which are now, and which could have existed under the Christian name, and then demonstrate that this is true of each and everyone of them. Such a treatise would fill so many volumes as to seem endless.

6. But you ask me for a handbook, that is, a book that can be carried in the hand, and not one to load your book-case. Now then, to return to those three things by which, as I have said, God is to be worshipped—faith, hope, and charity: it is easy to say what is to be believed, what is to be hoped for, and what is to be loved. However, to refute the calumnies of those who think otherwise, requires more painstaking and more detailed instruction. And to impart such instruction, it will not suffice to place a small manual in one's hands; rather it will be necessary to enkindle a great zeal in one's heart.

CHAPTER 2

The essentials of faith, hope, and charity are found summarized in the Creed and the Lord's Prayer.

7. Take, for example, the Creed and the Lord's Prayer. What is there that takes less time to hear or to read? What can be more easily committed to memory? Because the human race in consequence of sin was weighed down by great misery and stood in need of divine mercy, one of the Prophets, foretelling the time of God's grace, said: *And it shall come to pass that every one that shall call upon the name of the Lord shall be saved.*[11] For this reason you have the Lord's Prayer. But when the Apostle recalled this prophetic testimony in order to recommend this very grace, he added immediately: *But how shall they call on Him, in whom they have not believed?*[12] And for this reason you have the Creed. You will see that these two (the Creed and the Lord's Prayer)[13] contain those three matters under discussion: faith believes, and hope and charity pray. But

without faith the other two cannot exist; and thus faith likewise prays. On that account, of course, it has been **said**:
How shall they call on Him, in whom they have not believed?

8. But is it possible to hope for anything in which we do
not believe? We can, however, believe in something for
which we do not hope. Who in fact is there among the
faithful who does not believe in the punishment of the
wicked? Yet, he does not hope for it. Moreover, the man
who believes that such punishment threatens him and who
with shrinking of soul dreads it, is more correctly said to
fear than to hope. A certain poet, making a distinction
between the two things, says:

> Let him have hope besides fear.[14]

But this was not properly put by another poet, although a
better one:

> If I have availed to hope for such grief.[15]

Indeed, some grammarians refer to this instance to illustrate
diction improperly used and say: " He said *sperare* (to hope)
instead of *timere* (to fear)."

The object of faith is therefore evil as well as good, since
we believe in the existence of evil as well as of good. Still,
in either case faith itself is good, not evil. Moreover, faith
bears on things past, present, and future. We believe, for
instance, that Christ died, which fact happened in the past.
We believe that He sits at the right hand of the Father,
which fact is of the present moment. We believe that He will
come to judge, which event belongs to the future. Again,
faith extends to those things which pertain both to ourselves
and to others. For example, everyone believes that he once
began to exist and that he was not from eternity. He believes

the same of other persons and things. Nor is it only of other men, but of angels as well, that we believe many things pertaining to religion.

Hope, however, deals only with things that are good and which lie only in the future and which have a relevance to him who is said to entertain it. Since this is true, faith must on these grounds be distinguished from hope, both as a term and as a concept. What is common to faith and hope is that the object of both is something unseen. Indeed, in the Epistle to the Hebrews, to which illustrious defenders of the Catholic rule of faith have turned for support, faith is defined as *the demonstration of things not seen.*[16] However, when a man asserts that he believes, that is, bases his act of faith not on some one's word, not on witnesses, nor on any kind of reasoning, but only on the evidence of things present, he does not appear to be so foolish as to deserve to be taken to task or to be told: " You see; therefore you did not believe." Hence it can be maintained that it does not follow that a thing cannot be believed if it is the object of perception. Still, it is better to call faith, as the Holy Scriptures [17] have taught, that which concerns itself with things unseen.[18]

Concerning hope, the Apostle likewise says: *Hope that is seen, is not hope. For what a man seeth, why doth he hope for? But if we hope for that which we see not, we wait for it with patience.*[19] When, therefore, we believe that good things are to come to us, this means nothing else than that we hope for them.

What, now, shall I say of love, without which faith avails nothing? Neither can hope exist without love. Again, as the Apostle James says: *The devils also believe and tremble;* [20] but they neither hope nor love. Rather, believing that what we hope for and love will come to pass, they fear. For this reason the Apostle Paul approves and commends *faith that worketh by charity*,[21] which assuredly cannot exist without hope. Consequently, there is no love without hope, no hope without love, and neither hope nor love without faith.[22]

CHAPTER 3

The Triune God is the author of all being, but not the cause of evil.

9. When, therefore, you ask what we should believe in matters of religion, the answer is to be found not by exploring the nature of things, as was done by those whom the Greeks call physicists.[23] Nor need we be fearful if a Christian should fail to know some things about the force and number of the elements; about the motion and order and eclipses of the stars; about the form of the heavens; about the species and natures of animals, plants, stones, fountains, mountains; about the reaches of space and time; about the signs of approaching storms, and a thousand-and-one things which those men discovered or thought they had discovered. For even they, excelling by their great genius, burning with the love of research and free to indulge in it, investigating some things by the aid of human conjecture and searching out others by means of historical research, have not found out all things. And as to their vaunted discoveries, these more often are mere opinion than certain knowledge.[24]

For the Christian it is enough to believe that the cause of all created things, in heaven and on earth, visible or invisible, is none other than the goodness of the Creator, who is the one and true God; that there is no being whatsoever but God Himself or what comes from Him; that God is a Trinity, that is to say, the Father, the Son begotten of the Father, and the Holy Spirit proceeding from the same Father, but one and the same Spirit of the Father and the Son.[25]

10. By this Trinity, supremely and equally and unchangeably good, all things were made; but they were not made supremely and equally and unchangeably good. Nevertheless, they are all good, even taken individually; and then taken as a whole, they are very good,[26] since it is their totality that constitutes the marvellous beauty of the universe.

11. And in this universe even that which is called evil, being properly ordered and put in its place, sets off the good to better advantage, adding to its attraction and excellence as compared with evil. As even the infidels admit, the omnipotent God,

primal Power of the world,[27]

being Himself supremely good, could not permit anything evil in His works, were He not so all-powerful and good as to be able to bring good even out of evil.[28] But what is that which is called evil, but the privation of good? To illustrate: in animal bodies diseases and wounds are nothing but the loss of health. And when a cure is effected, it is not a case of those evils, that is, of the diseases and wounds which once were present, now leaving the body and taking up their abode elsewhere. Rather, they simply cease to exist. For the wound or disease is in no sense a substance, but is only the defect of a bodily substance. For the body itself is the substance, and consequently something good, in which those evils occur, namely, the loss of that good which is called health. So, too, whatever failings there are in the soul are privations of natural goods. When these imperfections are remedied, they are not transferred elsewhere; but as they disappear in the restored condition, they simply cease to exist.[29]

CHAPTER 4

The relativity of all created goodness.

12. Every being therefore is good, since He who is the Creator of all being whatever is supremely good. But because unlike their Creator they are not perfectly and unalterably good, the good which is in them can be both lessened and increased. But to lessen the good is to give rise to evil. However, to whatever extent it may be lessened, granting the continuance of the being, something of good must remain if the being itself is to continue in existence. For, no matter what the nature of the being may be, or how insignificant it may be, the good which gives it existence cannot be destroyed unless the being itself be destroyed. For good reason, then, do we esteem an incorrupted being. But if a being is incorruptible as well, entirely incapable of being destroyed, then beyond question it is all the more worthy of esteem. However, when corruption sets in, its corruption is an evil, because it deprives the being of some sort of good. For, if it deprives the being of no good, it does it no injury. But it does do injury; therefore it deprives it of good. As long, then, as a being suffers corruption, there is in it some good of which it is being deprived; and by the very fact that something of the being remains that can no longer be corrupted, the being evidently proves to be incorruptible, attaining this great good through the process of corruption.[30] However, if the corruption does not cease, then neither does the being cease to possess the good of which corruption can still deprive it. And should the corruption consume the being utterly and entirely, then no good will remain in it, because there will be no being left at all. Wherefore, corruption cannot destroy the good without destroying the being itself. Every being therefore is good. It is a great good if it cannot be corrupted; a small good, if it can. But only the foolish and ignorant man can deny that it is a good. If the being is destroyed by corruption, the corruption itself ceases to be, as there is no being left in which it could exist.

13. It follows from this that where there is no good, there is nothing that can be called evil. But a good which lacks all trace of evil is wholly good. If some evil is present, then the good is a corrupted or faulty good. There can never be evil where there is no good.

From this we deduce the curious fact that, since every being so far as it is a being is good, when we say that a faulty being is an evil being, we seem to say only that evil is good, and that nothing but good can be evil, seeing that every being is good and that no evil is possible if the very thing which is evil is not a real being. There can therefore be no evil thing unless it be something good. And although this seems to be a contradiction in terms, the logic of this reasoning seems inevitably to force us to make this conclusion.

At the same time we must be careful not to incur that prophetic condemnation which reads: *Woe to those who call evil good, and good evil, who call darkness light, and light darkness; that call bitter sweet, and sweet bitter.*[31] And still the Lord says: *An evil man out of the evil treasure bringeth forth evil things.*[32] But what is an evil man if not an evil being, since man is a being? Now, if a man is a good thing because he is a being, what is an evil man if not an evil good? But when we distinguish between these two things, we find that neither is he an evil because he is a man, nor is he a good because he is wicked. Rather, we find that he is a good so far as he is a man, and an evil so far as he is wicked. Whosoever, therefore, says that to be a man is evil, or that to be wicked is good, comes under that prophetic condemnation: *Woe to those who call evil good, and good evil.* For such a man finds fault with the works of God, that is, with man, and he praises the defect of man which is iniquity. Every being therefore, even though it be imperfect, is good so far as it is a being; so far as it is defective, it is evil.

14. Wherefore, in these contraries known as good and evil the rule of the logicians that two contraries cannot be found simultaneously in the same thing, does not hold. The atmosphere is never at the same time dark and bright; no food or drink is at the same time sweet and sour; no body is at the same time and in the same place white and black, or deformed and shapely. And this is observed to hold true of many, indeed of nearly all, contraries, that they cannot exist simultaneously in one and the same thing.

However, though no one contends that good and evil are not contraries, not only can they be present at the same time, but evil simply cannot exist without the good or in anything except good, although good can exist without evil. A man or an angel, for instance, can exist without being unjust, but only a man or an angel can be unjust. So far as he is a man or an angel he is good; he is evil so far as he is unjust.

And these two contraries are so closely brought together, that if there were no good in what is evil, evil could have absolutely no existence, because corruption cannot have a place in which to exist or a source from which to spring, unless there be something that can be corrupted; and unless this something be good, it cannot be corrupted, for corruption is nothing but the destruction of good. Evil things therefore had their origin in good things, and unless they reside in good things, they do not exist at all.[33] There was no other source whence an evil being could have originated. If there were, then to the extent that it were a being it would unquestionably be good. And if it were an incorruptible being, it would be a great good; and again, even if it were a corruptible being, it could not possibly exist unless it were somehow good, for only by corrupting that good can corruption do it harm.

15. Now, when we say that evil arose from good, let it not be thought that this gives denial to the Lord's principle in which He stated: *A good tree cannot bring forth evil fruit.*[34] As Truth puts it: *Men do not gather grapes from thorns,*[35] simply because grapes do not grow on thorns. But we see that on good soil both vines and thorns can grow. In the same way, just as an evil tree cannot bring forth good fruit—good works, that is—so neither can an evil will. But from the nature of man, which is good, there can come a will which can be good or evil.

Nor was there any other source from which an evil will could originally take its beginning, except in the nature of an angel or a man, which was good. This the Lord Himself clearly shows in that same passage in which He spoke of the tree and the fruits, for He says: *Either make the tree good and its fruit good: or make the tree evil and its fruit evil.*[36] This is a sufficiently plain reminder that evil fruit does not indeed grow on a good tree, nor good fruit on an evil one, but that nevertheless from the ground itself of which He was speaking both kinds of trees could grow.

CHAPTER 5

The right Christian attitude towards profane learning.

16. Now then, when we find acceptable that verse of Maro's,

Happy he who hath availed to know the causes of things,[37]

we must not imagine that it is essential to the attainment of happiness to know the causes of the world's great physical phenomena hidden away in the most secret recesses of nature—

> why quakes the earth,
> And by what power the oceans fathomless
> Rise, bursting every bound, then sink away
> To their own bed [38]—

and all other such things. But we ought to know the causes of good and evil so far as it is given to man to know them in this life replete with mistakes and miseries, in order that we may be able to avoid them. We must indeed strive for that state of happiness where no trouble will annoy us nor error mislead us. Certainly, if it were our duty to know the causes of the physical phenomena, there is none that we should have to know better than those which affect our own health. But when in ignorance of them we have recourse to physicians, who is there that does not see to what extent the secrets of the heavens and the earth remain hidden from us, and what great patience we need in order to bear with ignorance?

17. Although we must shun error with the greatest possible care in important matters and unimportant ones as well, and although we can err only through ignorance of certain things, yet it does not follow that a person who is ignorant of a thing must then and there fall into error. He errs only when he thinks he knows what he does not know, for he accepts what is false as true, and herein lies the essence of error. However, very much depends on the character of the error made. Of course, in one and the same matter one rightly prefers the man who knows to the one who is ignorant, and the one who makes no mistakes to the one who does. But when the issues are different, that is, when one man knows one thing and another man knows something else, and the former knows what is useful, the latter what is less useful or even harmful: who would not in regard to the things the latter knows prefer the ignorance of the former? For there are some things which it is better not to know than to know.

Again, sometimes people realize advantages from going astray—on the beaten path, that is, not on the path of morals. This once happened to me. I took the wrong way at a crossroad, and because of my mistake I did not pass by the place where an armed body of Donatists [39] lay in ambush for me. And so it chanced that I arrived at my destination in a roundabout way. When I learned of the trap they had set for me, I congratulated myself on having made the mistake and gave thanks to God for it. [40] Who then would have hesitated to prefer such an errant wayfarer as myself to the robber who had made no error about the roads? Perhaps it was for this reason that a certain unhappy lover speaking through that prince of poets said:

When I saw, how was I undone! How that
fatal error swept me away! [41]

For there is also such a thing as a mistake which is good,

one that not only does no harm but actually brings about some advantage.

But a more profound consideration of truth is this: to err is only to regard that as true which is false and that as false which is true, to hold that as certain which is uncertain and that as uncertain which is certain—whether false or true; and this is just as ugly and unbecoming in the soul as we deem it beautiful and becoming when in speaking or in giving our assent we say *Yea, yea—no, no.*[42] Surely, for this reason too the life we lead is a wretched one, that if it is not to be lost, error is sometimes indispensable to it. But that other life cannot be so—of course it cannot—that life where Truth itself is the life of our soul, and where no one deceives and no one is deceived.[43]

However, in this life men do deceive and are deceived, and they are more wretched when by lying they deceive than when by believing liars they themselves are deceived. Yet, to such an extent does a rational being shrink from falsehood and, as far as possible, endeavor to shun error, that even those who love to deceive do not themselves wish to be deceived. For the liar does not think that he himself errs, but rather that he leads into error the one who believes him. And he actually does not err in the matter which he covers up by a lie, if he himself knows the truth. But in this he is deceived, that he thinks the lie does him no harm; for every sin harms him who commits it more than the one against whom it is committed.

CHAPTER 6

The morality of lying.

18. But at this point there arises a very difficult and complicated question to which, since the need for an answer was urgent, I have already done justice in a large book: [44] is it ever the duty of a good man to tell a lie? Some, for example, go so far as to contend that on occasion it is a good and pious deed to commit perjury and to speak falsely about matters pertaining to the worship of God and about the nature of God Himself.[45] However, it seems to me that every lie is truly a sin, although it makes a great difference with what intention and in what matter a man lies. For the sin of him who lies in order to give help is not the same as that of one who lies in order to do harm. Nor does the man who by lying sends a traveller on the wrong road do as much harm as the one who by lying deceit perverts the way of life.

Of course, no one can be put down as a liar who says something false while believing it to be true, since obviously as far as he himself is concerned, he does not deceive but is being deceived. Hence, too, a man who through carelessness accepts the false as true is not guilty of lying, though he may sometimes be charged with rashness. On the other hand, though, a man is subjectively a liar who says what is true while thinking it to be false. For, so far as his intention is concerned, since he does not express what he thinks, he fails to tell the truth, even though what he does say should prove true; and there simply is no way of absolving a person from the charge of lying who without knowing it tells the truth with his lips while knowingly he lies in his heart. Hence, if we consider not the things themselves about which something is said, but only the intention of the speaker, the one who unwittingly says what is false while thinking it to be true is a better man than the one who unwittingly says what is true while intending in his conscience to deceive. For the former does not think one thing and say another, whereas the latter, whatever may be the factual content of what is said by him, "keeps one thing locked away in his heart and another ready on his lips"; [46] and this constitutes the real evil of lying.

But in a consideration of the things themselves that are said, it makes a great difference in what matter a man lies or is deceived. For whereas to be deceived is a lesser evil than to deceive as far as the individual intention is concerned, yet it is far more tolerable to lie in matters that have no connection with religion than to be deceived in those things without the knowledge and belief of which the worship of God is impossible. To illustrate, let us weigh these examples: one man lies stating that some dead person is still alive; another, being deceived, believes that Christ will die again at some distant time in the future. Would it not be incomparably better to lie like the former, than to be deceived like the latter? And would it not be a far less evil to lead a man into the former error than to be led by anyone into the latter?

19. In some things, then, we are deceived with consequent great harm, while in others little harm is done. Again, sometimes no harm at all results, and at times the deception turns even to our advantage. It is, for instance, with great harm to himself that a man is deceived by not believing in what leads to eternal life or by giving credence to things which lead to eternal death. But another is deceived with little harm to himself who by accepting as true what is false involves himself in some temporal troubles, but bringing to them patience born of faith turns them to good use—the case, for example, of some one taking a bad man to be good and suffering some injury from him. Again, one who believes a bad man to be good in such a way as to suffer no harm from him is none the worse for having been deceived, nor does he fall under that prophetic denunciation: *Woe to those who call evil good.*[47] For this is to be understood as having been said about the things that make man become evil, not about the men themselves. Hence, the man who calls adultery good stands justly accused by that word of the Prophet. But one who calls an adulterer good, believing him to be chaste and not knowing him to be an adulterer, is deceived not with regard to principles concerning good and evil, but only as to the secrets of human behavior. He simply calls this man good because he believes him to possess a quality which he knows is good, maintaining all the while that an adulterous man is bad and a chaste man good; though in this instance he considers the man to be good because he does not know that he is an adulterer and therefore not a chaste man.

And again, if through an error a man escapes a calamity, as I related had once happened to me while on a journey, then even some good comes to him from his error. But when I affirm that in certain instances a man is deceived without any harm to himself or with even some advantage accruing to him, I do not claim that his error is in itself not an evil or that it is to some extent good; but that by making the mistake, that is, due to the error itself one thing did not happen and another did, and because of this, evil did not materialize in the one case while good resulted in the other.

But error, considered in itself, is an evil: a grave evil in grave matters, a small evil in small matters—yet always an evil. For who except in error can deny that it is an evil to approve the false as true or to condemn the true as false, or to hold the uncertain as certain and the certain as uncertain? But it is one thing to believe a man to be good who is actually bad, which is a mistake; it is another thing not to suffer a new evil from this evil, as when a bad man who was believed to be good does us no harm. In like manner it is one thing to think that we are on the right road when we are not, and another to derive some good from the evil of this mistake, such as that of being saved from the ambush of wicked men.

CHAPTER 7

Augustine explains his philosophy of error and refutes the skepticism of the Academy.

20. I must confess I do not know whether errors such as the following and others like them should also be termed sins: [48] when a man thinks well of a bad person, not knowing what sort of a character he really is; or when in place of those things which we ordinarily perceive through the bodily senses similar phenomena occur which, actually perceived through the spirit, are referred to the body, or actually perceived through the body, are referred to the spirit—a case in point being the illusion of the Apostle Peter who, when suddenly freed by the angel from locks and chains, thought he was having a vision; [49] or when in material things themselves what is rough is thought to be smooth, or what is bitter is considered to be sweet, or what is malodorous is held to be fragrant; or when we mistake the passing of a wagon for thunder; or when we confuse two men who look very much alike, as often happens with twins—inspiring one of our great poets to write of

that error dear to parents.[50]

Nor do I propose to solve a very knotty question which perplexed the subtle thinkers of the Academy: [51] whether a wise man should give his assent to anything at all, confronted as he is by error, should he approve as true what is false; for according to these men all things are either obscure or uncertain. That is why during the early days of my conversion I wrote three volumes, that my progress might not be hindered by objections blocking, so to speak, the doorway.[51] Certainly it was necessary to remove that sense of the hopelessness of attaining to truth which apparently finds support in the arguments of the Academics. Now, among them every error is considered to be a sin, and this they contend can be avoided only by withholding assent altogether. In fact, they say, whosoever assents to things uncertain commits an error. Nothing is certain in human experience because of the impossibility of seeing through the sham that falsehood puts on. And even if one's assumption should happen to be true, they will dispute its truth by arguments extremely subtle but at the same time shameless.

However, among us *the just man liveth by faith*.[52] But take away assent, and you take away faith, since without assent one can believe nothing. And there are truths which may not be understood, but unless they are believed, it will be impossible for us to attain to the happy life, which is no other than life eternal. But I do not know whether we should argue with people who are unaware not only that they are to live forever, but even that they are alive now, and who even say that they do not know what they cannot but know. For evidently no one can be ignorant of the fact that he is alive, because if he is not alive he is incapable of even being ignorant, since not only to know but also not to know postulates a living being. But they of course imagine that they avoid error by not granting the fact that they are alive, when by the very mention of "erring" they prove themselves to be alive, for a dead man cannot err. As, then, it is not only true, but certain as well that we are alive, so there are many other things both true and certain; away, therefore, with the idea that the refusal of assent in such cases should be called philosophy and not madness!

21. In some matters it is of no consequence for our attainment of God's kingdom whether or not they are believed, or whether they are true, or held to be true, or whether they are actually false. To be in error concerning them, that is, to mistake one thing for another, is not to be judged a sin; or, if sin it is, it is a very small and light one.[53] Once for all, then, whatever its character and magnitude, such an error has nothing to do with the way that takes us to God—the faith of Christ *that worketh by charity*.[54]

That "error," for instance, concerning the twins, so "dear to parents," was no deviation from this way. Nor did the Apostle Peter deviate from this same way when, thinking he was having a vision, he so mistook one thing for another, that he did not distinguish the real bodies in the midst of which he was from the images of bodies among which he thought himself to be, until the angel by whom he was liberated had departed from him. Nor did the Patriarch Jacob depart from this way when he thought that his son, who was still living, had been slain by a beast.[55] In these and similar false notions we are deceived, with our faith in God remaining intact, and we go astray without departing from the way that leads to Him.

But, though these errors are not sins, still they are to be classed with the evils of life, which so yields to vanity [56] that here we accept the false as true, reject the true as false, and hold the uncertain for certain. Although these things do not touch upon that true and certain faith by which we tend towards eternal life, yet they do have to do with that misery in which we still abide. In very truth, we should in no wise be deceived by any faculty of soul or body if we were already enjoying that true and perfect bliss.

22. But every lie must be called a sin because it is man's duty, not only when he knows the truth but also when, being human, he errs or is deceived, to speak what is in his mind, whether this be really true or only thought to be true, whereas it is not.[57] But everyone who lies says the opposite of what is in his mind, and that in order to deceive. Surely, language was appointed not that by it men should deceive each other, but that through its instrumentality one man might make known his thoughts to another. Hence, to use language for the purpose of deception and not for what it was appointed, is sin.

And we must not think that because we can on occasion help others by lying, some lies are for that reason not sinful. For this we could as well do by stealing, when, for example, something is taken secretly from a rich man who does not sense the loss, and is presented as a gift to a poor man who appreciates it as a benefit; but no one would for this reason claim that such theft was not a sin. We could possibly do the same by committing adultery, when, for instance, some woman seems likely to die of love unless we give in to her, whereas if she lived, she might repent and be cured; but no one would claim that therefore the adultery is not a sin. If therefore we justly esteem chastity, where has truth offended, that for the benefit of another, chastity may not indeed be violated by the commission of adultery, whereas violation of truth by telling lies is tolerated?

Undeniably men who do not lie except to promote man's welfare have made great strides on the way to goodness. But what is justly praised or even accorded a temporal reward in this their progress is their good will, not their lie. It is enough that their lie should be pardoned; it should not be praised, particularly in the heirs of the New Testament to whom it is said: *Let your speech be yea, yea—no, no; and that which is over and above these, is of evil.*[58] Because of this evil which never ceases to steal in upon us during this earthly life of ours, the coheirs of Christ themselves say: *Forgive us our debts.*[59]

CHAPTER 8

Angels and men freely brought about their own ruin. Man is saved only by the grace of God.

23. Having discussed these problems with the brevity that the present treatise requires, we must now look into the causes of good and evil, to the extent at least that is sufficient for the way leading to the kingdom where there will be life without death, truth without error, bliss without fear. And here we cannot doubt at all that the cause of the good things which are ours is God's goodness alone, and that the cause of evil is the defection of the will in a being mutably good— first it was the will of an angel, then that of man—from the immutable good.[60]

24. Here we have the first evil to befall rational creation, that is to say, its first privation of good. After that there crept in even against man's will ignorance of things to be done and a craving for things that are harmful. And as companions to these came error and pain. Again, when these two latter evils are felt to be imminent, the state of the soul seeking to escape them is called fear. Furthermore, when the mind realizes the objects of its desires and because of error fails to perceive how harmful or empty they are, it is either fascinated by a morbid delectation or even transported with silly joy. From these diseased fountains—fountains, not of abundance, but of want—flows all the woe that is the portion of rational beings. **25.** Yet, in the midst of such evils these beings could not lose their desire for happiness.

Now, these are evils common to both men and angels whom God in His justice condemned because of their wickedness. But in addition man has received a penalty peculiar to himself, in that he is also punished with death of the body. For God had threatened man with the penalty of death,[61] should he sin. He gave him free will, so as still to guide him by His command and to deter him by the menace of death; and He placed him in the happiness of Paradise, in a life of security,[62] as it were, whence, provided he preserved his innocence, he was to rise to better things.

26. Having sinned, he was banished from that place, and by his sin he laid upon all his descendants, whom he had vitiated in himself as their source, the penalty of death and condemnation. As a result all the children born of him and his spouse who had led him into sin and was condemned together with him—children born through carnal lust as a retribution in kind for the act of disobedience—contracted original sin. Because of this sin they were drawn through a variety of aberrations and sufferings to that final unending punishment together with the rebel angels, their corrupters and masters and companions. Thus, *by one man sin entered into the world, and by sin death; and so death passed upon all men, in whom all have sinned.*[63] By the " world " the Apostle in that passage of course means the whole human race.[64]

27. And so the matter stood. The whole mass of condemned [65] human nature lay prone in evil, indeed, wallowed in it, and precipitated itself from one evil into another; and having aligned itself with the group of angels that had sinned, it was, like them, paying the well-deserved penalties for an impious rebellion. For certainly the just anger of God is reflected in whatever the wicked freely do through blind and uncontrolled lust, and in whatever punishments they are made to suffer against their will—known and unknown to others. But the goodness of the Creator does not indeed cease to administer even to the bad angels life and vitality, without which they would cease to exist. Nor does He cease to create and endow with life the seed of men, though born of a vitiated and condemned stock, to harmonize their members, to quicken their senses throughout the periods of time and the reaches of places, and to provide them with nourishment. For He deemed it better to bring good out of evil [66] than not to permit any evil to exist at all.

And assuming it to have been God's will that there should be absolutely no rehabilitation in the case of men, as there was none on the part of the wicked angels: would it not have been just if the being that had deserted' God, that abusing its endowment had trampled under foot and transgressed the law of its Creator when it could so very easily have kept it, that had obstinately turned away from His light, defiling the image of the Maker which it bore, and had maliciously and deliberately broken with the wholesome subjection of legislation—would it not have been just if such a being had been abandoned by God in its entirety and unto eternity and made to undergo everlasting punishment, as it deserved? Certainly God would have done this, were He only just and not also merciful and had He not chosen to give proof far more striking of His unmerited mercy by setting free those who were undeserving of it.[67]

CHAPTER 9

The Angels who remained loyal to God were confirmed in grace. Men can be restored to God's love not by their own merits but only by the grace of God.

28. After some of the angels, then, had through wicked pride deserted God and had been cast from their heavenly abode on high down into the lowest darkness of this air,[68] the remaining number dwelt with God in eternal bliss and holiness. For these other angels were not descended from one angel who had sinned and had been condemned. Hence, the original evil did not chain them, like men, to inheritance or guilt and deliver them over to merited punishments. On the contrary, once he who became the devil had together with his partners in infamy become arrogant, and because of this arrogance had been cast down, the other angels remained closely united in holy obedience to the Lord; and they received what those others had not possessed—a sure knowledge by which they were made certain of their everlasting and unfailing steadfastness.[69]

29. And so it pleased God, the Creator and Governor of the universe, that, since not all the multitude of angels had

deserted Him and perished, those who had fallen away
should remain in eternal perdition, while those who had
remained loyal to Him when the others forsook Him should
rejoice in bliss with absolute certainty that it was to be theirs
forever.

But the remainder of rational creation, mankind, having
perished in its totality under the weight of sin and punishments both original and personal, was to make up from its
redeemed members the loss which diabolical ruin had caused
to the angelic commonwealth. For such is the promise made
to the saints who rise again, that they will be equal to the
angels of God.[70] Thus, the heavenly Jerusalem,[71] our Mother,
the City of God, will not be robbed of her citizens, but will
perhaps reign over an even greater number. We do not of
course know the number of either the saints or of the unclean
demons whom the children of that holy Mother who seemed
barren on earth,[72] will replace in order to abide forever in
the peace which the demons lost.[73] However, the number of
those citizens, as it stands at the present or as it will be, is
present to the mind of the Maker who *calleth those things
that are not, as those that are,*[74] and who *ordereth all things
in measure, and number, and weight.*[75]

30. But can these members of the human race to whom
God promised deliverance and a place in the eternal kingdom,
be saved by the merits of their works? That is out of the
question. For what good work can one do who is ruined,
except so far as he has been delivered from his ruin? Can he
do so by the free determination of his will? That, too, is
out of the question. For it was by the evil use of his free will
that man destroyed both himself and his free will.[76] When,
for instance, a man kills himself, he is of course alive in the
act; but once he has killed himself, he no longer lives, nor is

he able to restore himself to life. So, too, when by free will sin was committed, sin being the conqueror, free will was lost; *for by whom a man is overcome, to the same also is he bound as slave.*[77]

This is certainly the mind of the Apostle Peter. And since this is true, what sort of liberty, I ask you, can the bondslave possess except the liberty to sin? For he serves freely who freely does the will of his master. Hence, he who is the servant of sin is free to sin. And therefore he will not be free to do what is right until, freed from sin, he begins to be the servant of justice.[78]

This is what constitutes true liberty—the joy experienced in doing what is right. At the same time it is a holy servitude arising from obedience to precept. But whence is man, sold and held in bondage, to have that liberty to do good, unless He buy him back who said: *If therefore the Son shall make you free, then you shall be free indeed?*[79] But before man begins to be in this state, how could anyone take glory in a good work as though proceeding from his free will, when he is not yet free to do what is right? Puffed up with silly pride, he would only be boasting. But this the Apostles reproves, saying: *By grace you are saved through faith.*[80] **31.** And lest they (the Ephesians) should arrogate to themselves their own faith at least, and not understand that it was given to them by God, the same Apostle, who says in another place that he had *obtained mercy of the Lord to be faithful,*[81] here also added, saying: *and that not of yourselves, but it is the gift of God; not of works, that no man may glory.*[82] And lest good works be thought to be wanting in the faithful, he added again: *For we are His fashioning, created in Christ Jesus in good works, which God hath prepared that we should walk in them.*[83]

Consequently, we shall then be made truly free when God fashions us, that is, forms and creates us, not as men, which He has already done, but as good men, which He now does by His grace, in order that we may be *a new creature in Christ* [84] according to the words: *Create a clean heart in me, O God.* [85] Of course, as regards the physical, human heart, God had already created this.

32. Again, in order that no one should boast, not indeed of his works, but of the free choice of his will, as if any merit had its origin in himself and the very freedom to do good had been bestowed upon him as a just reward, let him listen to what the same herald of grace says: *For it is God who worketh in you, both to will and to accomplish according to His good will;* [86] and elsewhere: *So then it is not of him that willeth, nor of him that runneth, but of God that showeth mercy.* [87] On the other hand, when a man is old enough to use his reason, beyond doubt he cannot believe or hope or love unless he wills to do so, nor obtain the palm of God's heavenly calling unless he decides to run for it. In what sense then is it *not of him that willeth, nor of him that runneth, but of God that showeth mercy,* unless it be that *the will* itself, as Scripture says, *is made ready beforehand by the Lord?* [88] Otherwise, if *it is not of him that willeth, nor of him that runneth, but of God that showeth mercy* was said because the action is from both, that is, from the will of man and from the mercy of God, then we accept that saying, *it is not of him that willeth, nor of him that runneth, but of God that showeth mercy,* as if it meant: "the will of man alone does not suffice if the mercy of God be not also present." But then neither does the mercy of God alone suffice if the will of man is not also active.

And again, if *it is not of man that willeth, but of God*

that showeth mercy is rightly said for the reason that the
will of man alone does not suffice, why then could not the
converse also be rightly said: " It is not of God that showeth
mercy but of man that willeth "—because the mercy of God
alone does not suffice? But if no Christian will dare to say:
" It is not of God that showeth mercy, but of man that
willeth," lest he utterly contradict the Apostle, it follows that
the saying, *it is not of him that willeth, nor of him that
runneth, but of God that showeth mercy*, is rightly understood to mean that the entire work is to be credited to God,
who both readies the will to accept assistance, and assists the
will once it has been made ready.[89]

The good will of man does in fact precede many of God's
gifts, but not all. Among those which it does not precede, it
also is included. Thus in the Holy Scriptures we read both:
His mercy shall prevent me [90] and *Thy mercy will follow
me*.[91] This mercy is prevenient to the unwilling to make him
will; it follows the willing that he may not will in vain.
Why, for instance, are we admonished to pray for our
enemies who certainly do not will to live virtuously, if not
that God should effect in them also the will to do so? [92]
Again, why are we exhorted to ask that we may receive,[92a]
unless it be that He through whom it happens that we will,
should grant what we will? We therefore pray for our
enemies, that the mercy of God may predispose them as it
also predisposes us; we pray for ourselves, that His mercy
may follow us.[93]

CHAPTER 10

The God-Man alone redeems our fallen race.

33. And so mankind was held in just condemnation and all men were children of wrath. Of this wrath it is written: *For all our days are spent; and in Thy wrath we have fainted away. Our years shall be considered as a spider.*[94] And Job also said of this wrath: *For man born of woman is short-lived and laden with wrath.*[95] And the Lord Jesus, too, said of this same wrath: *He that believeth in the Son, hath life everlasting; but he that believeth not the Son, does not have life; but the wrath of God abideth on him.*[96] He did not say " it will come," but, " it abideth." For every man is born with it; and therefore the Apostle says: *For we, too, were by nature children of wrath, even as the rest.*[97]

Since men lay under this wrath because of original sin, all the more grave and deadly as they added to it other and greater sins, there was need for a mediator, that is, for a reconciler who by the offering of a unique sacrifice, of which all the sacrifices of the Law and the Prophets were but the shadows, should placate that wrath. Hence, the Apostle says: *For if, when we were enemies, we were reconciled to God by the death of His Son; much more, being now reconciled by His blood, shall we be saved from wrath through Him.*[98]

But when God is said to be angry, we do not impute to Him any perturbation such as exists in the soul of an angry man; rather, His vengeance, which is always just, has received the name " anger," the word having been taken over by analogy from human emotions.[99] The fact therefore that through the Mediator we are reconciled to God and receive

the Holy Spirit so as to be changed from enemies into sons—
*for whosoever are led by the Spirit of God, these are the sons
of God* [100]—this is the grace of God through Jesus Christ
our Lord.

34. To say of this Mediator all the great things that
would be fitting would take entirely too long: in fact, man
could not do justice to the subject. For example, who could
explain in adequate terms this single statement that *the Word
was made flesh, and dwelt among us,* [101] so that we should
believe in the only Son of God the Father Almighty, born
of the Holy Spirit and the Virgin Mary? Yes, indeed, just
so was the Word made flesh—by the Godhead assuming flesh,
not by the Godhead having been changed into flesh. By
" flesh," moreover, we are here to understand " man," the
part being taken for the whole. [102] In this sense was it said:
Because by the works of the law no flesh shall be justified, [103]
that is to say, " no man." It certainly is not right to say that
in that assumption anything was lacking in His human
nature, except that it was wholly free from every bond of
sin. [104] It was not such a nature as is born of the two sexes
through the lust of the flesh and with the debt of sin, the
guilt of which is washed away by regeneration. Rather, it
was a nature such as was proper to one born of a virgin, one
whom a mother's faith and not her lust had conceived. And
if only in His birth her virginity had been destroyed, from
that moment He would not have been born of a virgin, and
the whole Church would proclaim falsely, which God forbid,
that He was born of the Virgin Mary. [105] This Church,
imitating His Mother, daily gives birth to His members, and
she, too, remains a virgin. [106] Read, if you will, my letter on
the virginity of the Holy Mary, sent to a distinguished gen-
tleman whose name I mention with respect and affection,
Volusianus. [107]

35. Wherefore, Christ Jesus, the Son of God, is both God and man. He is God before all ages; man in our own time. He is God because He is the Word of God, for *the Word was God.*[108] But He is man because in His own Person there were joined to the Word a rational soul and a body. Therefore, so far as He is God, He and the Father are one; [109] but so far as He is man, the Father is greater than He.[110] Since He was the only Son of God, not by grace but by nature, in order that He should also be full of grace He became likewise the son of man; and the one selfsame Christ results from the union of both.[111] For, *being in the form of God, He thought it not robbery* [112] *to be* what He was by nature, that is, *equal with God; but He emptied Himself, taking the form of a servant,*[113] neither losing nor diminishing the form of God.

And thus He became less and still remained equal, being both in one, as has been said. In the one instance this was because He was the Word; in the other, because He became man. As the Word He is equal to the Father; as man He is less. The one Son of God, He is at the same time Son of man; the one Son of man, He is at the same time Son of God. Being God and man did not make Him two sons of God,[114] but one Son of God: God without beginning, man with a definite beginning—our Lord Jesus Christ.[115]

CHAPTER 11

The Excellency of God's grace becomes manifest through the Incarnation.

36. Here above all the grace of God manifests itself with striking sublimity. For, what had the human nature of the man Christ merited that it should be so singularly taken up into the unity of the Person of the only Son of God? What good will, what striving for good ends, what good works had gone before, in virtue of which this man would become one person with God? Had He been man before this, and was this unique grace bestowed upon Him because He had singularly merited to become God? Not at all. From the moment that He began to be man, He did not begin to be other than the Son of God, the only Son of God; and because of God the Word which by assuming Him had become flesh, He was truly God.[116]

Just as every human being is one person, that is, a rational soul and a body, so, too, is Christ one Person, the Word and man. And why was so great glory bestowed upon human nature—gratuitously of course, as there were no antecedent merits?[117] For the sole reason that here all who would consider the matter in the light of faith and reason might have a clear manifestation of God's great and extraordinary grace; and that thus men might understand that they are justified from their sins by the same grace by which the man Christ was made incapable of any sin whatever. And thus did the angel greet His Mother when he announced to her His future birth: *Hail,* said he, *full of grace*; and a little later he added: *Thou hast found grace with God.*[118] And she is called full of grace and said to have found favor with God, for she was to become the mother of her Lord, indeed, of the Lord of all. Again, when the Evangelist John said of Christ Himself: *And the Word was made flesh, and dwelt among us,* he added: *and we saw His glory, the glory as it were of the only-begotten of the Father, full of grace and truth.*[119] When he says, " the Word was made flesh," he means, " full of grace "; when he says, " the glory of the only-begotten of

the Father," he means, "full of truth." Indeed, it was
Truth Itself, the only-begotten Son of God, not by grace but
by nature, that gratuitously took upon Himself man in so
perfect a union of Person that He Himself became also the
Son of man.

37. For truly the same Jesus Christ, the only-begotten,
that is, the only Son of God our Lord, was born of the Holy
Spirit and the Virgin Mary. And certainly the Holy Spirit is
the Gift of God,[120] which gift is in truth itself equal to the
Giver. Therefore, the Holy Spirit also is God, not inferior
to the Father and the Son. Hence, again, what does the
fact that the birth of Christ according to His human nature
is of the Holy Spirit show forth if it be not grace? For, when
the Virgin asked the angel how that which he announced to
her should come to pass, as she knew not man, the angel
answered: *The Holy Ghost shall come upon thee, and the
power of the most High shall overshadow thee. And therefore also the Holy which shall be born of thee shall be called
the Son of God.*[121] And when Joseph wanted to send her
away because he suspected her of adultery, knowing as he
did that she was with child—but not by him, he received this
answer from the angel: *Fear not to take unto thee Mary thy
wife, for that which is conceived in her is of the Holy
Ghost;*[122] that is to say, "what you suspect to be of another
man, is of the Holy Spirit."

CHAPTER 12

Christ is not the Son of the Holy Spirit, though He is born of Him. His birth of the Holy Spirit again proclaims the gratuitous character of divine grace.

38. But are we therefore to conclude that the Holy Spirit is the father of the man Christ? That as God the Father generated the Word, so the Holy Spirit generated the man, and that from these two substances there resulted the one Christ—the Son of God the Father so far as He is the Word, and the Son of the Holy Spirit so far as He is man? That the Holy Spirit became the father of Christ by begetting Him of the Virgin Mary? Who would dare to make such a statement? Nor is it necessary to show by argumentation how many other absurdities would follow: the statement is of itself so absurd that no believer's ears can bear to hear it. Hence, as we confess, our Lord Jesus Christ, who of God is God, but as man was born of the Holy Spirit and [123] the Virgin Mary, is in virtue of both substances, namely the divine and the human, the only Son of God the Father Almighty, from whom proceeds the Holy Spirit.

How can we therefore say that Christ was born of the Holy Spirit, if the Holy Spirit did not beget Him? Is it because He made Him? For, though so far as our Lord Jesus Christ is God, *all things were made by Him,*[124] evidently, so far as He is man, He Himself was made, as the Apostle says: *He was made of the seed of David, according to the flesh.*[125] But since that creature which the Virgin conceived and brought forth, though it belonged to the Person of the Son alone, was made by the entire Trinity whose works are inseparable, why then should the Holy Spirit alone be men-

tioned as having made it? Or is it that when one of the
Three is mentioned in connection with some work, the entire
Trinity is to be understood as doing that work? Yes, so it is,
and it could be proved by examples.[126] But we must not
remain too long on this subject.

What we are really concerned with is this: how can we say
" He was born of the Holy Spirit," when He is in no sense
the Son of the Holy Spirit? Just because God made this
world, it would not be right to say that the world is the son
of God, or that it was born of God; rather, we say that it was
made or created or fashioned or constituted by Him, or how-
soever else we might properly put it. Here, then, when we
confess that Christ was born of the Holy Spirit and the
Virgin Mary, it is difficult to explain why He is not the Son
of the Holy Spirit as well as the Son of the Virgin Mary,
when He was born both of Him and of her. Beyond a doubt,
the fact is that He was not born of the Holy Spirit as His
father in the same sense that He was born of the Virgin as
His mother.

39. Consequently, we must not grant that whatever is
born of something is forthwith to be called a son of that
thing. Let me pass over the fact that a son is born of a
man in a sense different from that in which a hair or a louse
or a stomach worm is born of him—none of which is a son.
This I pass over, I say, as an ugly comparison with a subject
of such moment. But again, certainly no one would rightly
call those men sons of water who are born of water and the
Holy Spirit; though they are justly called the sons of God
the Father and of Mother Church.[127] In like manner, then,
He who was born of the Holy Spirit is the Son of God the
Father, not of the Holy Spirit.[128] For what we said about
the hair and the other things serves to remind us that not

everything which is born of another can be called the son of
that of which it is born. Conversely, it does not follow that
all who are called a man's sons should also be said to have
been born of him, as there are those who are sons by adoption. Moreover, there are so-called "sons of hell," [129] not
because they have been born of hell, but because they have
been prepared for it, as "the sons of the kingdom" [130] are
prepared for the kingdom.

40. Since, therefore, a thing may be born of another and
still not in such a way as to be its son, and again, since not
everyone who is called a son has been born of him whose
son he is called, that very manner by which Christ was born
of the Holy Spirit, but not as His son, and of the Virgin
Mary as her son, most assuredly tells us something about the
grace of God, by which a man without any antecedent merits
was at the very beginning of His human existence joined to
God the Word unto so great a unity of person, that the same
one who is the Son of man should be the Son of God, and the
same one who is the Son of God should be the Son of man;
and thus, in the adoption of His human nature grace became,
as it were, that Man's very nature, [131] to the exclusion of every
possibility of sin. This grace was therefore to be signified
through the Holy Spirit, because He is Himself so perfectly
God as to be called also the Gift of God. [132] To give an adequate presentation of this, if indeed it could be done at all,
would be matter for a very lengthy discussion.

CHAPTER 13

The sinless Christ freely atoned for our sins and purifies our souls in the sacrament of baptism. Are the sins of parents visited upon their children?

41. Christ was therefore begotten and conceived of no lust of carnal concupiscence. For this reason He brought with Him no original sin. Again, by the grace of God He was most intimately united in a wonderful and ineffable way in one Person of the Word, the Only-Begotten of the Father, His Son not by grace but by nature; and for this reason He was also free from personal sin. Yet, because of *the likeness of sinful flesh* [133] in which He came, He was Himself called sin, destined as He was to be sacrificed in order to wash away sin. [134] In fact, under the Old Law sacrifices for sins were called sins. [135] And He, of whom those sacrifices were but shadows, was Himself truly made sin. Hence, when the Apostle said, *For Christ we beseech you to be reconciled with God,* he immediately added: *Him, who knew no sin, He hath made sin for us, that we might be the justice of God in Him.* [136] He does not say, as some faulty copies read: " He who knew no sin did sin for us," as though Christ Himself sinned for us; but he said: *Him, who knew no sin,* Christ, that is to say, God—to whom we are to be reconciled—*hath made sin for us,* that is, a sacrifice for sin by which we might be reconciled to God.

He, then, was sin, as we are justification; but this justification is not our own but God's, not in ourselves but in Him, just as He was sin, not His own but ours; and that it was enrooted not in Himself but in us, He demonstrated in *the likeness of sinful flesh* in which He was crucified. Thus, since sin was not in Him, He wishes to die, so to speak, to sin while dying in the flesh in which was the likeness of sin; and He who Himself had never lived the old life of sin wished by His Resurrection to seal our new life, rising up again from the old death by which we had been dead in sin.

42. This is precisely what is meant by the great sacrament of baptism which is solemnized among us: all who attain to this grace should die to sin, just as He is said to have died to sin because He died in the flesh, that is, in the likeness of sin; and they should live by being born again from the font, as did Christ by rising again from the sepulchre.[137] The age of a person makes no difference. **43.** For, as no one, from the infant newly born to the old man bent with age, is to be barred from baptism,[138] so there is no one who in baptism does not die to sin. But infants die to original sin only, while adults die also to all those other sins which by their evil lives they have added to the sin they contracted at birth.[139]

44. But even these latter are often said to die to sin, although without doubt they do not die to one sin but to all the many sins which they committed personally in thought, word, and deed. The evident reason is that the plural number is often indicated by the singular, as in the words of the poet:

They fill its belly with the armed soldier [140]—

whereas they did this with many soldiers. And we read in our own Scriptures: *Pray therefore to the Lord that He may take from us the serpent.*[141] The writer does not say " serpents," as he should, since the people were being plagued by them. And there are countless other instances of the same kind. When, on the other hand, that single original sin is spoken of in the plural number, as when we say that infants are baptized "unto the remission of *sins*" instead of saying "unto the remission of *sin*," then we have the converse figure of speech in which the singular is expressed by means of the plural. Thus, when Herod was dead, the Gospel says: *For they are dead that sought the life of the child,*[142] and not, "*he* is dead." And in Exodus we read: *They made to themselves gods of gold,*[143] although the people had made but one calf, of which they said: *These are thy gods, O Israel, that have brought thee out of the land of Egypt*[144]—thus also putting the plural for the singular.

45. However, even in that one sin which *by one man entered into the world*[145] and passed on to all men, and because of which even infants are baptized, a plurality of sins can be discovered if we break it down, so to speak, into its component parts. For in it there is pride, since man chose to be under his own dominion rather than under God's; also blasphemy, since man refused to believe God; and murder, for he rushed headlong into death; and spiritual fornication, since the innocence of the human soul was corrupted by the seduction of the serpent; and theft, since man appropriated to himself forbidden food; and avarice, since he craved for more than sufficed for his needs; and whatever else may be found by diligent reflection to have been involved in the commission of this one sin.

46. It is said with a real basis of probability that children are involved not only in the sin of our first parents but also in the sins of their own parents of whom they are born. For that divine sentence, *I shall visit the iniquities of the fathers upon their children,*[146] certainly applies to them before they come under the New Testament through regeneration. And it was this Testament that was foretold when Ezechiel said that the sons should not in the future bear the sins of their fathers and that no longer should that byword apply to Israel: *Our fathers have eaten sour grapes, and the teeth of the children are set on edge.*[147]

Every one, therefore, who is born again, is born again in order that whatever sin was in him at the time of birth should be absolved. For the sins which are committed later on through evil actions can be washed clean by penance,[148] as we see done after baptism. And for this reason alone was the rebirth instituted, because our birth is sinful and sinful to such a degree that even one who had been born in lawful wedlock said: *I was conceived in iniquities; and in sins did my mother nourish me in her womb.*[149] Nor did he say, as he might have done correctly, " in iniquity " and " in sin "; but he chose to say " iniquities " and " sins," because in that one sin which passed on to all men and which was so great that by it human nature was changed and subjected to the necessity of dying, many more sins, as I explained above, are found; and because there are other sins—those of our parents—which cannot, it is true, change our nature in the same manner, but which nevertheless involve the children in guilt, unless the gratuitous grace and mercy of God intervenes.

47. But as to the sins of a man's other parents, the ancestors through whom he traces his lineage from Adam to his own father, a discussion might well be raised. Is that man at his birth implicated in all their evil-doings and their multiplied original transgressions, so that the later he is born the worse off he is? Or does God threaten to visit the sins of the parents upon their posterity only unto the third and fourth generations, because with merciful restraint He does not permit His wrath to encompass the guilt of more distant forebears? He does not want those who do not receive the grace of regeneration, eternally condemned as they are, to be crushed under too heavy a load, as they would be if they were forced to contract as their own the sins of all those who from the beginning of the human race preceded their own parents, and to pay the penalty due to them. Whether or not a more painstaking study and interpretation of Holy Scripture might yield some other solution of so momentous a problem, is a question which I dare not answer offhand.[150]

CHAPTER 14

Our regeneration in baptism is made possible by the Sacrifice of Christ. He is our model. He will come to judge us on the last day.

48. Still, that one sin, committed in a place and a state of such great happiness, a sin of such enormity that through one man the whole human race was originally and, I might say, radically, condemned, is absolved and blotted out only through *the one Mediator of God and man, the man Christ Jesus,*[151] who alone could be so born as not to need to be reborn.

49. Those who were baptized by the baptism of John, by whom He also was baptized, were not regenerated. But through the ministry of this precursor who kept saying, *Prepare ye the way for the Lord,*[152] they were made ready for Him in whom alone they could be born again. For, His baptism is not by water alone, as was John's, but also by the Holy Spirit.[153] Thus, whosoever believes in Christ is born again of that Spirit, of whom Christ also was born, though

He needed not to be born again. Hence, too, those words of the Father spoken over Him at His baptism: *This day have I begotten thee*,[154] pointed not to that one day in time on which He was baptized, but to that of changeless eternity, to show us that this man was identical with the Person of the Only-Begotten. For, where a day neither begins with the close of yesterday, nor ends with the beginning of tomorrow, there it is eternal today.

He, therefore, chose to be baptized in water by John, not in order that any sin of His might be washed away but that His great humility be made manifest.[155] For baptism certainly found nothing in Him that needed to be washed away, just as death found nothing in Him that needed to be punished. Hence, it was by strict justice and not by a mere imposition of force that the devil was crushed and conquered, for, as he had most unjustly caused Him to be slain who was free from all guilt of sin, most justly should he lose through Him those whom he held in subjection because of the guilt of sin. To both, then, that is, to baptism and death, did Christ submit Himself, following a special plan—not because of a pitiable necessity but by His own free act of taking pity [156] on us—by which one Man was to take away the sin of the world, as one man had brought sin into the world, that is, upon the whole human race.

50. But there is this difference: whereas the one man brought one sin into the world, this Man took away not only that one sin, but also all the others which He found added to it. The Apostle therefore says: *Not as it was by one sin, so also the gift. For judgment indeed was by one unto condemnation; but grace is of many offences, unto justification.*[157] Evidently, that one sin which man contracts at birth would, even if it were his only one, make him liable to condemna-

tion; but grace justifies from many transgressions man who
has committed, besides the one sin which at birth he drew
upon himself in common with all others, many sins wholly
his own.

51. However, when the Apostle again says a little farther
on: *As by the offence of one, unto all men to condemnation;
so also by the justice of one, unto all men to justification of
life,*[158] he indicates clearly enough that there is no one born
of Adam who is not subject to condemnation, and no one
freed from condemnation who is not born again in Christ.

52. And when in the opinion of the Apostle the chapter
in his letter concerning punishment through one man and
concerning grace through the Other had received adequate
attention, he next spoke of the great mystery of holy baptism
as bound up with the Cross of Christ; and this he does in
terms that make us understand baptism in Christ as nothing
but an image of Christ's death, and that Christ's death on the
Cross is nothing but an image of the remission of sin. Just
as real as was His death, so real is the remission of our sins; [159]
and just as real as was His Resurrection, so real is our justification. For the Apostle says: *What shall we say, then? Shall
we continue to sin, that grace may abound?* [160] For in the
preceding he had said: *Where sin abounded, grace did more
abound.*[161] And therefore he asked himself the question:
whether to obtain abundance of grace one should continue
in sin. But he answered, *God forbid*; and added: *For we
that are dead to sin, how shall we live therein?* [162]

Next, to show that we are dead to sin, he said: *Know you
not that all we, who are baptized in Christ Jesus,*[163] *are baptized in His death?* [164] If, then, the fact that we are baptized
in the death of Christ shows that we are dead to sin, then

surely infants, too, at their baptism in Christ die to sin, because in His death they are baptized. No exception was made in the statement, *All we, who are baptized in Christ Jesus, are baptized in His death*; and the reason for the statement was to prove that we are dead to sin.

But to what sin do infants die in their regeneration other than that which they bring with them at birth? Consequently, what follows now in the letter of the Apostle pertains also to them: *We are therefore buried together with Him by baptism into death; that as Christ is risen from the dead by the glory of the Father, so we also may walk in newness of life. For if we have been planted together in the likeness of His death, we shall be also in the likeness of His Resurrection. Knowing this, that our old man is crucified with Him, that the body of sin may be destroyed, to the end that we may serve sin no longer. For he that is dead is justified from sin. Now if we be dead with Christ, we believe that we shall live also together with Christ; knowing that Christ rising again from the dead, dieth now no more, death shall no more have dominion over Him. For in that He died to sin, He died once; but in that He liveth, He liveth unto God. So do you also reckon, that you are dead to sin, but alive unto God, in Christ Jesus.*[165]

Now, this is what the Apostle had set out to prove, that we must not remain in sin in order that grace should abound. He had said: *For we that are dead to sin, how shall we live therein?* And, to prove that we are dead to sin, he had added: *Know you not that all we, who are baptized in Christ Jesus, are baptized in His death?* And thus he closes this entire passage just as he began it. In fact, he brought in the death of Christ in such a way as to say that even He died to sin. But to what sin, if not to the flesh in which there was not sin, but only the likeness of sin, wherefore it was called sin? And so to those baptized in Christ's death, in which not only adults but also infants are baptized, he says: *So*—that is, as Christ did—*do you also reckon that you are dead to sin, but alive to God, in Christ Jesus.*

53. Whatever was done, then, in the crucifixion of Christ, in His burial, in His resurrection on the third day, in His ascension into heaven, in His enthronement at the right hand of the Father, was so done in order that these things might serve as a model for the Christian life which is lived here below—a model based not on mystical language alone, but on deeds as well. Thus, in view of His crucifixion it was said: *And they that are Jesus Christ's have crucified their flesh, with its passions and concupiscences;* [166] in view of His burial: *For we are buried together with Him by baptism into death;* [167] in view of His resurrection: *That Christ is risen from the dead by the glory of the Father, so we also may walk in newness of life;* [168] in view of His ascension into heaven and His enthronement at the right hand of the Father: *But if you be risen with Christ, seek the things that are above; where Christ is sitting at the right hand of God. Mind the things that are above, not the things that are upon earth. For you are dead; and your life is hid with Christ in God.* [169]

54. But as to our belief concerning what Christ will do in the future, namely, that He will come from heaven to judge the living and the dead, this does not pertain to our life as we live it here; for neither is it a part of what He did on earth, but of what He will do at the end of the world. It is to this that the Apostle referred when he goes on to say: *When Christ shall appear, who is your life, then you shall also appear with Him in glory.* [170]

55. Now, the statement that He *shall judge the living and the dead* [171] may be taken in two ways. Either we may understand by the living those who are not yet dead and whom His advent will find still abiding in the flesh, and by the dead those who before His coming have departed from the body or will so depart; or we may understand by the living the just, by the dead the unjust—the just also being subject to judgment. Indeed, sometimes the judgment of God is used with an implication of evil, as, for instance: *But they that have done evil* (shall come forth) *unto the resurrection of judgment;* [172] and sometimes with an implication of good, as is stated in *Save me, O God, by Thy name, and judge me in Thy strength.* [173] In fact, it is through the judgment of God that a division of the good and the evil is made, so that the good who are to be freed from evil and not to be left to perish with the wicked, may be set apart at His right hand. Wherefore the Psalmist exclaimed: *Judge me, O God and*—as if to explain what he had just said—*distinguish my cause from the nation that is not holy.* [174]

CHAPTER 15

The Holy Spirit and the Church Triumphant and Militant. Some problems concerning the angels.

56. Now, having spoken of Jesus Christ, the only Son of God our Lord, in a manner consonant with the brevity of the Creed, we add that we believe likewise in the Holy Spirit, thus completing the Trinity, which God is. Next, mention is made of the Holy Church. We are thus given to understand that rational creation belonging to the free Jerusalem [175] was to be put after the mention of the Creator,

that is, of the sublime Trinity; for, of course, whatever has
been said of the man Christ pertains to the oneness of the
Person of the only-begotten Son of God. Hence, the correct
sequence of the Creed demanded that the Church be sub-
joined to the Trinity, as a dwelling to its Inhabitant, as a
temple to God,[176] and a city to its Founder. And here it is
the whole Church that is to be understood—not that part
only which sojourns on earth, praising the name of the Lord
from the rising of the sun to its setting [177] and chanting a
new song [178] of deliverance from its ancient captivity; but
that part also which always was in heaven, which always
remained loyal to God, its Creator, and did not experience
the woe that springs from a fall. This part, consisting of
the holy angels, abides in perpetual bliss and helps, as it
should, the other part which is still in exile; [178a] for both
parts will be one in the fellowship of eternity, and even now
are one in the bond of charity, the whole Church having
been instituted for the purpose of worshipping God. Wherefore, neither the whole Church nor any of its parts wishes to
be worshipped as God or to be God to anyone belonging to
the temple of God, which is built up of the gods [179] whom
He, the uncreated God, created.

And consequently the Holy Spirit, were He a creature and
not the Creator, would certainly be a rational creature, for
this is the highest creature; on that account He would not be
placed in the Rule of Faith [180] before the Church: He Himself would evidently belong to the Church, to that part of
it which is in heaven. Nor would He have a temple, for He
Himself would be part of the temple. But a temple He does
have, concerning which the Apostle says: *Know you not
that your bodies are the temple of the Holy Ghost, who is
in you, whom you have from God?* [181] And on this subject

he says in another passage: *Know you not that your bodies are the members of Christ?* [182] How then, since He has a temple, should He not be God? Or how can He be less than Christ, whose members are His temple? Nor is His temple different from the temple of God, since the same Apostle says: *Know you not that you are the temple of God?* And, as if to prove this, he added: *And that the Spirit of God dwelleth in you?* [183] God, then, dwells in His temple; not the Holy Spirit alone, but also the Father and the Son, who says of His body by which He was made the Head of the Church on earth so *that in all things He may have the primacy: Destroy this temple, and in three days I will raise it up.* [184] Therefore, the temple of God, that is, of the sublime Trinity as a whole, is the Holy Church—the Church everywhere, in heaven and on earth.

57. Now, as to the Church which is in heaven, what can we say about it except that no wicked one is found in it, and that no one has fallen away from it, nor will fall away from it, since the time that *God spared not the angels that sinned—* as the Apostle Peter writes—*but, casting them out, delivered them into the dark prisons of hell, to be reserved unto judgment?* [185]

58. And how is that most blessed and supernal society of angels constituted? What differences of pre-eminence obtain among the angels to account for the fact that while all go by the general name of "angels," yet archangels are found there? Thus, we read in the Epistle to the Hebrews: *But to which of the angels said He at any time: " Sit on my right hand "?* [186] Here the writer certainly made clear that all without exception are angels. Again, are these archangels to be called hosts, so that the passage, *Praise ye Him, all His* *angels: praise ye Him, all His hosts,*[187] would be the same as if it read: " Praise ye Him, all His angels: praise ye Him, all His archangels " ? And what difference is there among the four terms under which the Apostle seems to have ranged the whole celestial body, when he said: *Whether thrones, or dominations, or principalities, or powers?* [188] Let those who are able tell us about this, but only if they can prove what they assert; as for me, I confess my ignorance concerning these things. Why, not even of this am I certain: whether the sun and the moon and the other stars do not belong to this same society—though ever so many do hold them to be merely luminous bodies without sensation or intelligence.[189]

59. Moreover, who will explain with what sort of bodies angels appeared to men so that they could not only be seen, but even touched? And again, how is it that not through bodies of flesh and blood, but by means of a spiritual force they present certain visions not to the bodily eyes but to the spiritual ones, that is, to the mind, or communicate something not to our ears from without but from within the soul, they being present even there, as is written in the book of the Prophets: *And the angel that spoke in me, said to me.*[190] He does not say, " spoke *to* me," but, " *in* me." Or again, how do they appear to men in their sleep and speak to them through dreams, as we read in the Gospel: *Behold, the angel of the Lord appeared to him in his sleep, saying?* [191]

By these manifestations the angels in a way indicate that they do not have tangible bodies; and this raises a very difficult problem: how, for example, did the Patriarchs wash their feet? [192] And how did Jacob wrestle with the angel, really exchanging grips with him, as he did? [193] When such questions are raised and each one guesses at the answers as best he can, our intellects are exercised not without profit, as long as the discussion is kept within proper bounds and the mistake of presuming to have knowledge when there is none, is avoided. After all, what need is there of affirming or denying with finality these matters and others like them, when no stigma attaches to our knowing nothing about them? [194]

CHAPTER 16

Satan. The brotherhood of the Church Triumphant and the Church Militant. Eternal peace.

60. The greater is the need to discern and recognize Satan when he transforms himself, as it were, into an angel of light,[195] lest he should deceive and seduce us into doing something sinful. Of course, when he deceives the bodily senses without diverting the mind from that true and right judgment by which a man leads the life of faith, the life of religion is not endangered; or when, pretending to be good, he does or says the things that befit good angels, even should he then be believed to be good, the delusion caused is not dangerous or fatal to Christian faith. When, however, through these borrowed means he begins to lead us into his own ways, then there is need of great vigilance in order to see through him and refuse to follow him. But how many people are there who are prepared to escape all his death-dealing wiles, unless God watches over them and keeps them from going astray? The very difficulty of this matter is helpful in this sense that it prevents a person from placing his trust in himself or in some other man; rather, God becomes this trust to all His own. And certainly, no man of piety denies that this is most expedient for us.

61. This part of the Church, therefore, which consists of the holy angels and hosts of God will become known to us as it really is, when we are finally united to it in the common possession of everlasting happiness. But the other part which, separated from it, sojourns on earth, is the better known to us because we ourselves belong to it and because it consists of human beings such as we ourselves are. This part it was that was redeemed from all sin by the sinless Mediator, and its voice it is that says: *If God be for us, who is against us? He that spared not His own Son, but delivered Him up for us all.*[196] Evidently, Christ did not die for the angels. Still, whatever was done through His death for the redemption of man and his deliverance from evil, was also done for the angels, considering that in a sense men return to friendship with them from the enmity which sin had created between mankind and the holy angels; and considering further that this redemption of mankind resulted in a replacement of the losses sustained in that angelic catastrophe.[197]

62. And certainly the holy angels, taught by God, the eternal contemplation of whose truth constitutes their bliss, know how great a supplementary number the full count of their citizenry demands from humankind. For this reason the Apostle says: *To re-establish all things in Christ that are in heaven and on earth, in Him.*[198] The things that are in heaven are re-established when that which was lost from among the angels is restored from the ranks of men; and the things that are on earth are re-established when those men who are predestined to eternal life are redeemed from their ancient corruption. And so by that matchless sacrifice in which the Mediator was immolated and which one sacrifice was symbolized by the many victims under the Law, the heavenly things are set at peace with earthly things, and earthly things with heavenly things; [199] because, as the same Apostle says, *in Him, it hath well pleased the Father, that all fullness should dwell; and through Him to reconcile all things unto Himself, making peace through the blood of His Cross, both as to the things that are on earth, and the things that are in heaven.*[200]

63. This peace, as Scripture says, *surpasseth all understanding,*[201] and cannot be known by us until we have attained it. For how can things in heaven be made at peace except with us, that is, by coming into harmony with us? There, it is evident, there is abiding peace, both in all the intelligent creatures among themselves and between them and their Creator. And this peace, as has been said, *surpasseth all understanding;* our understanding, that is, not theirs who always see the face of their Father. However great our human understanding may be, it is only fragmentary: *We see now through a glass in a dark manner.*[202] But when we shall be *the equals of* God's *angels,*[203] then, even as they, *we shall see face to face,*[204] and we shall have the same calm affection for them as they have for us, because we shall love them as much as we are loved by them.

And so the peace that is theirs will be revealed to us, because ours will be the same as theirs and as great as theirs, nor will their peace any longer surpass our understanding. But the peace of God which will there pervade us will doubtless surpass our understanding and theirs as well; for to the extent that a rational creature is happy, his happiness comes from God, and not conversely. Accordingly, it is better that the passage, *The peace of God that surpasseth all understanding,* be so understood that in the word "all" not even the intellect of the holy angels should be excepted, but only God's; obviously, His peace does not surpass His own understanding.

CHAPTER 17

The guilt and the remission of sin.

64. But the angels are in accord with us even now when our sins are remitted. Hence, in the plan of the Creed the remission of sins is placed after the mention of the Holy Church. For it is by this that the Church on earth stands; it is through this that what *was lost and is found* [205] does not perish. Of course, an exception is made by the gift of baptism, which is an antidote against original sin, so that what is contracted by birth should by a second birth be taken away; though it, too, takes away whatever actual sins have been committed prior to it in thought, word, and deed. Except, therefore, for this great gift of remission, whence begins man's renovation and by which all guilt, inherited and superadded, is forgiven, the rest of our life from the time we have the use of reason, is not lived without the need of remission of sin, however vigorous its progress in holiness. For, as long as the sons of God live subject to death, they remain in conflict with death. And, although it is truly said of them: *Whosoever are led by the Spirit of God, they are the sons of God,* [206] still their response to the promptings of the Spirit of God and their advance as sons of God towards God is conditioned by the fact that as the sons of men they are also moved by their own spirit, weighed down as it is by the corruptible body, [207] and under the influence of certain human passions fall away to their own selves, and thus commit sin. But a distinction must be made according to the gravity of the case: it does not hold that because every crime is a sin, therefore every sin is a crime. [208] We can say, then, that the life of holy men, as long as they remain in this mortal life, can be found to be without crime; but, says the great Apostle, *if we say that we have no sin, we deceive ourselves, and the truth is not in us.*[209]

65. However, in the Holy Church the remission of even crimes themselves, no matter how great they may be, by God's mercy need not be despaired of by those who do penance according to the gravity of their sins. But when the crime committed is such that the sinner is also cut off from the body of Christ,[210] we must consider in the act of repentance not so much the measure of time as the measure of sorrow; for, *a contrite and humbled heart God will not despise.*[211]

But since the sorrow of one man's heart is for the most part hidden from another and does not come to the knowledge of others through words or any other signs, when it is manifest to Him who is addressed with: *My groaning is not hidden from Thee,*[212] those who govern the Church with good reason appoint times of penance, that satisfaction may be made also to the Church in which the sins are remitted. For outside the Church there is no remission of sins. She received as her very own the pledge of the Holy Spirit,[213] without whom no sin whatever is remitted, so that those to whom sins are remitted receive life everlasting.[214]

66. It should be remembered that there is a remission of sins chiefly because of the future judgment. But even in this life the word of Scripture: *A heavy yoke is upon the children of Adam from the day of their coming out of their mother's womb until the day of their burial into the mother of all,*[215] is so true that we see even infants who have received the bath of regeneration tormented with the affliction of various kinds of evils. Thus we are given to understand that

the entire efficacy of the sacraments of salvation is directed
rather to the hope of goods to come than to the retention or
the attainment of present goods. So, too, there are many
things here on earth that apparently go unnoticed and un-
punished; but punishment for them is reserved for the future,
and it is not in vain that the day on which the Judge of the
living and the dead will come is specifically called the Day
of Judgment. On the other hand, some sins are punished
in this life and, provided they have been forgiven, certainly
will not visit harm upon us in the life to come. Hence,
speaking of certain temporal punishments inflicted upon
sinners in this life, in order that those whose sins are blotted
out may not have these punishments held over unto the
end,[216] the Apostle says: *For if we would judge ourselves,*
we should not be judged by the Lord. But whilst we are
judged, we are chastised by the Lord, that we be not con-
demned with this world.[217]

CHAPTER 18

Not all men are saved. Faith that works through love is
necessary for salvation. The purifying fire of grief and the
fire of Purgatory.[217a]

67. There are some people who believe that even those
who do not forsake the name of Christ, who are baptized by
His bath in the Church and are not cut off from her by any
schism or heresy, but who live in ever so great sins, never
washing them away by penance nor atoning for them by
almsgiving and persisting in them with utter pertinacity
down to the last day of their lives, will be saved by fire; and
although it is believed that such are punished with fire of

long duration in proportion to the enormity of the infamous crimes they have committed, the fire is not to be an ever-lasting one. However, men who, though Catholic,[218] believe this are deceived—so it seems to me—by a kind of humani-tarian benevolence. When we consult Divine Scripture, we receive a different answer. Moreover, I have written a book on this subject, entitled *Faith and Works.*[219] In it I have, God helping me, demonstrated to the best of my ability that according to the Holy Scriptures the faith that saves men is the faith which the Apostle Paul describes clearly enough, saying: *For in Christ Jesus neither circumcision availeth any thing, nor uncircumcision: but faith that worketh by charity.*[220] But if it works evil, and not good, then without doubt, as the Apostle James says, *it is dead in itself.*[221] And elsewhere he says: *If a man say he hath faith, but hath not works, shall faith be able to save him?*[222] And further, if a wicked man were to be saved by fire because of his faith alone, and if the words of the blessed Paul: *but he himself shall be saved, yet so as by fire,*[223] are to be understood in this sense, then faith without works is sufficient for salvation. False would be the statement of his fellow Apostle James, and false, too, that statement of the selfsame Paul: *Do not err: neither fornicators, nor idolaters, nor adulterers, nor the effeminate, nor liers with mankind, nor thieves, nor covetous, nor drunkards, nor railers, nor extortioners, shall possess the kingdom of God.*[224] If even those who continue in these crimes are nevertheless saved because of their faith in Christ, how, then, shall they not possess the kingdom of God?

68. But since most clear and patent testimonies of the Apostles cannot be false, that one obscure statement con-cerning those who build upon the foundation which is Christ not gold, silver, and precious stones, but wood, hay, and

stubble—for it is said of these that they will be saved by
fire, because due to the excellence of their foundation [225] they
will not perish—must be so understood as not to contradict
these clear testimonies.

Now, wood, hay, and stubble may not unreasonably be
taken to mean such an attachment to wordly things, things
licit enough in themselves, that their loss cannot but cause
grief in the soul. And since this grief burns, while Christ
remains the foundation in the heart—that is, provided nothing
is preferred to Him and provided the one who burns with
this grief nevertheless prefers to go without these things
which he loves so much, rather than to lose Christ—then one
is saved by fire. But if in time of temptation a man should
prefer to hold on to these temporal and worldly things rather
than to Christ, then he does not have Christ for his foundation; he is simply putting these things in first place, whereas
in a building nothing comes before the foundation. Further,
the fire of which the Apostle spoke in that passage is to be
understood as a fire through which both men must pass, that
is, both the man who builds gold, silver, and precious stones
upon this foundation, and the one who builds wood, hay, and
stubble; for, having said this, he added: *The fire shall try
every man's work, of what sort it is. If any man's work abide
which he hath built thereupon, he shall receive a reward.
If any man's work burn, he shall suffer loss; but he himself
shall be saved, yet so as by fire.*[226] It is therefore not the work
of the one only, but of both, that the fire will try.

Now, the trial of adversity is a kind of fire, and this is
clearly stated in another Scripture passage: *The furnace
trieth the potter's vessels, and the trial of affliction just men.*[227]
The fire referred to here does in the course of this life
precisely what the Apostle said; for instance, there is the one

who *is solicitous for the things that belong to the Lord, how he may please God*,[228] a man, therefore, who builds on Christ his foundation, gold, silver, and precious stones; whereas another *is solicitous for the things of the world, how he may please his wife*,[229] one, therefore, who builds on this same foundation, wood, hay, and stubble. The work of the former is not burned, because he has not loved things whose loss might have caused him grief; but that of the latter is burned, because things that are loved in possessing them are not lost without pain. But since even in this latter case the man prefers the alternative of going without these things to going without Christ and does not forsake Christ out of fear of losing them—though he grieve ever so much in losing them—*he is saved, yet so as by fire*, for he burns with grief over the things he loved and has lost; but it does not overwhelm or consume him, fortified as he is by the firmness and the indestructibility of his foundation.[230]

69. That something similar may take place after this life is not impossible. The question whether such is the case, is justified and may yield to a solution or remain in doubt: the question whether some of the faithful are saved by a sort or purgatorial fire,[231] and this later or sooner according as they have loved more or less the goods that perish. However, this has nothing to do with those of whom it was said that *they shall not possess the kingdom of God*,[232] unless having done commensurate penance they receive remission of their crimes.[233] I say "commensurate penance," meaning that they must not be barren of almsgiving. It is alms that Holy Scripture makes so much of, with the Lord stating in advance that on the mere basis of having been fruitful in these He will credit merit to those on His right hand, and that the absence of these alone will be imputed to those on His left, when He shall say to the former: *Come, ye blessed of my Father, possess you the kingdom*; but to the latter: *Go into everlasting fire.*[234]

CHAPTER 19

Our sins are forgiven through repentance, the Lord's Prayer, and through almsgiving. There are various kinds of alms-giving.

70. Of course, here there is need for caution. Let no one suppose that those unspeakable crimes the commission of which excludes from the kingdom of God, can be perpetrated daily and daily atoned for by almsgiving. By all means, life must be changed for the better, and because of past sins we need to be reconciled with God through almsgiving. But He is not to be bought off, so to speak, with a view to sinning at any time with impunity. For *He hath given no man license to sin,*[235] although in His mercy He does blot out sins that have been committed, if proper satisfaction for them is not neglected.

71. But as regards the everyday sins of a momentary and slight nature—and no one's life is without them [236]—for these the daily prayer of the faithful makes satisfaction. For they can say *Our Father who art in heaven,*[237] having already been born again to such a Father by water and the Holy Spirit. This prayer wipes out entirely the slight faults of every day. It likewise takes away those sins because of which the life of the faithful was for a time wicked, but by penance is at last changed for the better; the provision being that as sincerely as they say *forgive us our debts*—and the need of forgiveness is always present—so sincerely too do they say *as we also forgive our debtors*; [238] that is, provided what is said is also done. And to forgive a man who asks for pardon is actually the same as giving him alms.

72. For this reason the Lord's words: *Give alms; and behold, all things are clean unto you,* [239] hold good of all that is done through practical works of mercy. Hence, not only the man who gives food to the hungry, drink to the thirsty, raiment to the naked, hospitality to the stranger, shelter to the fugitive; who visits the sick and the shut-ins, ransoms the captives, carries the lame, leads the blind, comforts the sorrowful, heals the sick, points out the way to the lost, counsels the perplexed, and gives the necessaries of life to the poor—not such a man only, but also he who pardons the sinner truly gives alms. And so does the man who corrects with blows or restrains by any kind of disciplinary measure another over whom he has authority, at the same time forgiving from his heart the sin by which he has been wronged or insulted, or praying that it may be forgiven him. He is a giver of alms not only in that he forgives or prays, but also in that he reproves and administers punishment making for betterment; for in this he shows mercy. In truth, many good things are bestowed upon men against their will, when their interests and not their predilections are consulted. These men are found to be their own enemies, whereas their true friends are rather those whom they consider to be their enemies; and by way of mistake they return evil for good, whereas a Christian may not even return evil for evil.

There are, therefore, many kinds of alms, the giving of which helps us to obtain pardon for our sins; **73.** but none is greater than that by which we forgive from our heart a sin that some one has committed against us. There is no greatness in wishing well or even doing good to one who has done us no evil. It is a far nobler thing and it betokens goodness truly magnificent to love also your enemy and always to wish well and, when possible, do good to the man who wishes you evil and at every opportunity does you harm. Thus we heed God when He says: *Love your enemies; do good to them that hate you; and pray for them that persecute you.*[240]

But these injunctions are only for the perfect sons of God. All the faithful should indeed strive to make them their own and should by praying to God and by putting forth their best efforts and struggles endeavor to bring their souls up to this ideal. Seeing, then, that so great a good as this is not to be expected of so great a number as we believe are heard when it is said in prayer, *forgive us our debts, as we also forgive our debtors*,[241] beyond doubt the words of solemn agreement here implied are fulfilled when a man, not yet so perfect as to be ready to love his enemies, does grant pardon from his heart to one who has sinned against him and asks for pardon. For he certainly wishes to be pardoned when he requests it, praying and saying as he does, *as we also forgive our debtors*— that is: " Forgive our debts when we ask for forgiveness, as we also forgive our debtors when they ask for forgiveness from us." [242]

Again, when one has sinned against another and is moved by his sin to ask the other for pardon, he should no longer be deemed an enemy; and to love him now should not be so difficult as it was when he was still acting as an enemy. But the man who does not forgive from his heart another who regrets his offence and asks for pardon, must indeed not suppose that his own sins are forgiven him by the Lord. For Truth cannot lie. And what hearer or reader of the Gospel is there who does not know who it is that said: *I am the truth?* [243] It is the same who, when giving us the Prayer, forcefully drove home this sentence that He had put in, saying: *For if you will forgive men their offences, your heavenly Father will forgive you also your offences. But if you will not forgive men, neither will your Father forgive you your offences.* [244] Anyone who is not awakened by such thundering words is not asleep, but dead; though it is within His power to awaken even the dead.

CHAPTER 20

Almsgiving without purpose of amendment is useless.

75. Those, to be sure, who lead most wicked lives and make no effort to amend their lives and their ways, but amid all their degrading misdeeds continue to bestow alms, flatter themselves in vain with the Lord's words: *Give alms; and behold, all things are clean unto you.* [245] They do not understand the limited meaning these words have. But that they may understand, let them note to whom He said this. In the Gospel there is written: *As He was speaking, a certain Pharisee prayed Him, that He would dine with him. And He going in, sat down to eat. And the Pharisee began to say, thinking within himself, why He was not washed before dinner. And the Lord said to him: " Now you Pharisees make clean the outside of the cup and of the platter; but your inside is full of rapine and iniquity. Ye fools, did not He that made that which is without, make also that which is within? But yet that which remaineth, give as alms; and behold, all things are clean unto you."* [246] Are we to understand this to mean that to the Pharisees who do not have the faith of Christ all things are clean as long as they give alms, and give them in the manner determined by them, even though they do not believe in Christ nor are born again of water and the Spirit? As a matter of fact, all are unclean who are not made clean by the faith of Christ, the faith referred to in the words: *purifying their hearts by faith;* [247] and in those of the Apostle: *But to them that are defiled, and to unbelievers, nothing is clean; but both their mind and their conscience are defiled.*[248] How, then, could all things be clean to the Pharisees, if they gave alms but were not believers? Or how could they be believers, if they refused to believe in Christ or to be born again of His grace? And yet, what they heard is true: *Give alms; and behold, all things are clean unto you.*

76. But the person who wishes to give alms methodically should begin with himself and first give alms to himself. Almsgiving is plainly a work of mercy, and in all truth is it said: *Have pity on thy soul, pleasing God.*[249] It is for this purpose that we are born again, that we should please God, who is justly displeased with that which we contracted in being born. This is our first alms, one which we gave to ourselves when through the mercy of a compassionating God we looked after our wretched selves, acknowledging, as we did, that His judgment was just by which we were made wretched and concerning which the Apostle says: *Judgment indeed was by one unto condemnation;*[250] and giving thanks for His great charity, of which that same herald of grace says: *But God commendeth His love towards us; because when as yet we were sinners Christ died for us.*[251] And thus, by forming a correct judgment concerning our own misery and by loving God with the love which He Himself bestowed, it is possible for us to lead holy and upright lives. But while the Pharisees paid no attention to this judgment and this charity of God, they gave according to their custom of almsgiving tithes of even the very least of their fruits; [252] and so, in giving alms they did not begin with themselves and show mercy to themselves first. And it is concerning this order of showing love that it was said: *Thou shalt love . . . thy neighbor as thyself.*[253] When, therefore, He had rebuked them because they made themselves clean on the outside, but within were full of greed and wickedness, He admonished them to make clean their inward being by means of a special kind of alms, one which a man must give to himself first. *But yet*, He says, *that which remaineth, give as alms; and behold, all things are clean unto you.* Then, in order to make clear what it was He had admonished them to do, but which they took no care to do, and that they might not suppose Him to be unaware of their almsgiving, He said: *But woe to you, Pharisees!*[254] This was as if He said: "I have indeed admonished you to give alms, by which means all things might be clean to you. *But woe to you, because you tithe mint and rue and every herb*—and I know these alms of yours and you must not think that my admonitions have anything to do with them—*and pass over judgment and the charity of God.* By this kind of alms you could make yourselves clean from all inward impurity, so that even your bodies which you wash would be clean to you." For this is what is meant by " *all* things "— both inward and outward, as we read in another passage: *Make clean the inside, and the outside will become clean.*[255] But in order not to leave the impression that He had rejected those alms given from the fruits of the earth, He said: *These things you ought to have done*, in reference to judgment and the love of God, *and not to leave the other undone*, referring to the alms coming from the fruits of the earth.

77. Let them, therefore, not deceive themselves who think that by giving alms—and be they ever so generous, whether in money or in kind—they can purchase for themselves impunity to persist in the enormity of their crimes and in their moral rottenness. It is not that they simply commit these crimes: they are so attached to them that they would like to go on and on with them—if they could but do so with impunity! *But he who loveth iniquity hateth his own soul;* [256] and he who hates his own soul is not merciful but cruel to it. For by loving it according to the world, he hates it according to God. Consequently, if he wished to give alms to it and thus make all things clean to himself, then he would hate his soul according to the world and love it according to God. But no one gives any alms of any sort unless he receive what he gives from Him who is not in need of it. This is the sense of: *His mercy shall prevent me.* [257]

CHAPTER 21

The relative gravity of sins.

78. Now, what sins are light and what grave is a matter to be weighed not by man's judgment, but God's. Thus we see that for some sins allowance was made even by the Apostles. Such was the case, for instance, when the venerable Paul said to married people: *Defraud not one another, except by consent, for a time, that you may give yourselves to prayer; and return together again, lest Satan tempt you for your incontinency.* [258] Here this could possibly be considered as being no sin, that is, for married people to have intercourse not for the sake of procreating children—which is the purpose of marriage—but also for the sake of carnal pleasure, thus providing an escape for the incontinent weak from the deadly sin of fornication, or adultery, or any other form of uncleanness which it is shameful even to mention, but to which they might be seduced by lust through the temptation of Satan. It is possible, I said, that this should not be thought a sin, had Paul not added: *But I speak this by way of concession, not by commandment.*[259] And now, who will deny this to be a sin, when admittedly those who do this have only a concession made on apostolic authority to excuse them?

Another example in point is found in the statement: *Dare any of you, having a matter against another, go to be judged before the unjust, and not before the saints?*[260] And again: *If therefore you have judgments of things pertaining to this world, set them to judge, who are the most despised in the church. I speak to your shame. Is it so that there is not among you any one wise man, that is able to judge between his brethren? But brother goeth to law with brother, and that before unbelievers.*[261] Here, too, it might be thought that it is not a sin to bring suit against another and that sin is present only in wanting to have the case adjudged outside the Church, had not the Apostle at once followed this up with: *Already indeed there is plainly a fault among you, that you have lawsuits one with another.*[262] And lest anyone should excuse this, saying that he has a just cause and is suffering injustice which he wishes to have removed by the sentence of the judges, Paul straightway meets such thoughts and excuses by saying: *Why do you not rather suffer wrong? Why do you not prefer to be defrauded?*[263] Thus we are brought back to what the Lord said: *If a man will take away thy coat and contend with thee in judgment, let go thy cloak also unto him.*[264] And again: *Of him that taketh away thy goods, ask them not again.*[265] Therefore, He has forbidden His own to go to law with other men about worldly matters, and because of this teaching the Apostle says that to do so is a wrong. But when, notwithstanding, he permits such suits to be decided in the Church with brethren judging between brethren, while most sternly forbidding them outside the Church, it is evident that here again some allowance is made for the weakness of some brethren. Because of these sins and others like them, and of others again perhaps of even lesser moment and consisting of offences in words and thoughts, and because, as the Apostle James confesses, *in many things we all* offend,[266] we should pray to the Lord daily, saying often: *Forgive us our debts*; and let us not be lying in what follows: *as we also forgive our debtors.*

79. But there are some sins which would seem to be very slight, had they not been shown by the Scriptures to be more serious than is thought. For who would think that one who says to his brother *Thou fool*, is *in danger of hell-fire*,[267] did not He, Truth itself, say so? But for the wound He immediately supplied the remedy by adding the precept of brotherly reconciliation in the following words: *If therefore thou offer thy gift at the altar, and there thou remember that thy brother hath anything against thee*,[268] etc. Or again, who would think of the great sin involved in observing days and months and years and seasons, as do those who are willing or unwilling to begin anything on certain days or in certain months or years,[269] because, following the vain teachings of men, they believe in stated times as being lucky or unlucky,[270] were we not able to judge of the seriousness of this evil by the fear of the Apostle saying to such men: *I am afraid for you, lest perhaps I have labored in vain among you?*[271]

80. Add to this that sins, however grave and detestable they may be, once they become habit, are regarded as small sins or not sins at all. This goes so far, that such sins are not

even looked upon as something to be kept secret, but are
rather boasted of and published abroad—cases, therefore, in
which, as is written, *the sinner is praised in the desires of his
soul and the unjust man is blessed.*[272] In Sacred Scripture
wickedness of this sort is called a " cry." You have an example of this in the Prophet Isaias when he says of the evil
vineyard: *I looked that he should do judgment, but he did
iniquity; and not justice, but a cry.*[273] Whence also it is said
in Genesis: *The cry of Sodom and Gomorrha is multiplied,*[274]
because among these people such crimes were not only not
punished, but they were even a common, public practice—
sanctioned by law, as it were.

And in our own times many evils, though not the like of
those just mentioned, have so become matters of public custom, that not only dare we not excommunicate a layman, we
dare not even degrade a cleric for having committed them.[275]
Thus, when some years ago I was expounding the Epistle to
the Galatians, that very pertinent passage where the Apostle
says: *I am afraid for you, lest perhaps I have labored in vain
among you,*[276] forced me to exclaim: " Woe to the sins of
men, that we should shrink from them only when we are
not accustomed to them! But once we become inured to
them, though the Son of God shed His blood to wash them
away and though they be so great as to shut off completely
the kingdom of God from them, yet, seeing them so often,
we are led to tolerate them all, and tolerating them so often,
to commit many of them ourselves. Now grant, O Lord, that
we may not come to do all the things which we have not the
power to prevent! " [277] Some day I shall know whether im-
moderate grief did not get the best of me and make me
speak rashly.

CHAPTER 22

Two sources of sin: ignorance and weakness. Repentance is a gift from God. The sin against the Holy Spirit.

81. I shall now speak of what I have stated often before in other passages of my books.[278] We commit sin because of one of two reasons: either we do not as yet see what we ought to do, or we do not do what we know ought to be done. The first of these is the evil of ignorance; the latter, that of weakness. Against these we should of course fight; but we shall certainly be defeated unless we are helped by God not only to see what must be done, but also, sound judgment coming to our aid, to have the love of what is right triumph in us over the love of those things by which, desiring to possess them or fearing to lose them, we knowingly and willingly commit sin. In this latter case not only are we sinners—such we were already when we sinned through ignorance—but we are also transgressors of the law in that we do not do what we know beforehand ought to be done, or do what we know ought not to be done. Wherefore, not only should we pray for pardon when we have sinned, saying: *Forgive us our debts, as we also forgive our debtors*; but we should also pray for guidance that we may be kept from sinning, saying: *bring us not into temptation*.[278a] And we should pray to Him of whom it is said in the Psalm: *The Lord is my light and my salvation*.[279] As my light, He takes away my ignorance; as my salvation, He removes my weakness.[280]

82. Even penance itself, when according to the practice of the Church there is just cause for its being performed,[281] is frequently left undone because of weakness; for shame is only the fear of provoking displeasure when human esteem gives more satisfaction than the demands of justice, which leads a man to humble himself by doing penance.[282] It follows that God's mercy is needed not only when penance is done, but also in order that it may be done. Otherwise the Apostle would not say of certain men: *If peradventure God may give them repentance.*[283] And that Peter might be able to weep bitter tears, so the Evangelist tells us, *the Lord looked on Peter.*[284]

83. But the man who does not believe that sins are forgiven in the Church and therefore scorns this great largess of divine bounty and ends his days in such obstinacy of heart, is guilty of the unpardonable sin against the Holy Spirit,[285] through whom Christ forgives sins. This difficult question I have discussed as clearly as I could in a little book written on this one point.[286]

CHAPTER 23

The resurrection of the body.

84. Now, regarding the resurrection of the body—not a resurrection such as some have had only to die again, but a resurrection to eternal life as is that of Christ's own body—I am at a loss how to discuss this briefly and do justice to all the questions that are usually raised on the subject.[287] Nevertheless, no Christian may in any way doubt that the bodies of all men, those already born and those yet to be born, those who have died and those who will die, are to rise again.

85. First, then, there is the question concerning miscarriages, cases therefore of births taking place in the mother's womb, but not advancing to that stage in which a rebirth could take place.[288] If we are to assert a resurrection for them, this should at all events be found acceptable with regard to fetuses which are already developed.[289] However, in the case of fetuses that are still undeveloped, who would not rather hold that they perish like seeds that have not been conceived? On the other hand, who would dare to deny, though he may not venture to affirm it, that at the resurrection whatever was defective in the form will be supplied? Thus there would not be wanting the perfection which was to come in time, corresponding to the future absence of defects which otherwise times does bring about. Thus, too, nature would neither be deprived of anything which is its proper due and which time would have brought to it, nor, on the other hand, be marred by anything untoward and unfortunate which time does bring with it. What was not yet complete would be made whole, just as what has been marred will be restored.

86. And for this reason the question may be raised and made the subject of most profound discussion by eminent scholars, though I do not know whether man can find the answer at all: namely, just when does human life begin to exist in the womb? Does some form of latent life exist there before it manifests itself in the movements of a living being? For in the case of infants who are cut out limb by limb from the womb, lest if they be left there dead, they kill their mothers also: [290] simply to deny that such infants ever were endowed with life seems to be an all too rash presumption. But certainly, once a man begins to live, from that moment also it is possible for him to die. And if he dies, no matter where death befalls him, I cannot see how he is not to share in the resurrection of the dead.

87. And not even concerning monstrosities which, how-ever soon they may die, are born alive can we say that they will not rise again, or hold that they will rise again with their present deformities and not rather with bodies made per-fectly normal. God forbid that the double-limbed human being recently born in the Orient, of whom most trustworthy brethren gave an eyewitness report and concerning whom the presbyter Jerome of blessed memory left a written ac-count—God forbid, I say, that we should believe that there will rise again one person with double members, and not rather two individuals, which they would have been had they reached birth as twins.[291] And so in other cases: all births that are termed monstrosities because of the multiplica-tion or absence of certain members, or because of the presence of some extraordinary deformity, will at the resurrection be restored to the normal human shape in such a way that every soul will have its own body and not two bodies joined to-gether—no matter how closely these were knit together at birth. Each will possess separately all the members which constitute a complete human body.

88. More, with God the earthly matter out of which the flesh of mortal man is created does not perish. Whether it be resolved into dust or ashes, whether it be dispersed to the winds and skies, or whether it be converted into the sub-stance of other bodies or into the elements themselves, or whether it serve as food for beasts or even men and be changed into their flesh: in an instant it returns to that soul which first animated it [292] so as to make it become a human being and to make it live and grow.[293]

89. Now, then, the earthly matter which on the soul's departure becomes a corpse, will not at the resurrection be restored in such a way that those elements which disintegrated and were changed into this or that shape and form of other things, must necessarily return to the very same parts of the body to which they originally belonged; though they will return to the same body from which they were separated. Else, to suppose that the hair recovers all that so many shearings have taken away, and the nails all that frequent trimming has cut away, strikes the imagination as being a disfigurement so exaggerated and grotesque as to result in our not believing in the resurrection at all. But suppose, for example, that a statue made of some soluble metal were melted down by fire or crushed into powder or reduced to a shapeless mass, and an artist wished to restore the statue from the mass of its original material, it would make no difference to its completeness what particular particles of the material would be returned to any one part of the statue, as long as the restored statue recovered all the material of which it was originally composed. In like manner God, the Artist of marvellous and ineffable power, will with marvellous and ineffable speed restore our body from the totality of matter of which it originally consisted. Nor will it be of any importance for its restoration whether hairs return to hairs and nails to nails, or whether that portion of them which was lost be changed into flesh and taken back into other parts of the body: in His Providence the Artist sees to it that nothing unseemly results.

90. And again, it does not follow that because individuals differed in stature during life, that they will also differ in stature when they are brought back to life; nor that those who were thin will be thin, and those who were fat will return to life with their former obesity. But if it is in the Creator's plan that each should preserve in his new features his individuality and a recognizable likeness to his former self, while in the remaining physical endowment all should be equal, then all matter will be so disposed of in each that none of it will be lost; and what may have been wanting in some, will be supplied by Him who, as He willed it, was able to create even out of nothing.

But if in the bodies of those rising again there is to be a well-devised inequality, such as there is in voices which make up a full chorus, then the disposition of the matter of each man's body will be such as to give man a place in the angelic assemblage and to bring in nothing to jar upon their sensibilities. To be sure, nothing that is unseemly will be there; but whatever will be there, will be becoming; and this because anything that would be unbecoming, will simply not be.

91. The bodies of the saints will therefore rise again free from every defect, from every deformity, as well as from every form of corruption, encumbrance, or hindrance. In this respect their freedom of action will be as complete as their happiness; and for this reason their bodies have been called " spiritual," though undoubtedly they will be bodies and not spirits. For, just as we speak now of the body as being " animate," though as such it is a body and not a soul,[294] so, too, the body will then be spiritual, though as such it will be a body and not a spirit.

With regard to corruption, then, which now weighs down the soul, and with regard to vices by which *the flesh lusts against the spirit,*[295] there will then be no flesh, but body only, for bodies are said to be also in heaven. Wherefore it is said: *Flesh and blood shall not possess the kingdom of God;* and, as if to explain what has just been said, *neither shall corruption possess incorruption.*[296] What the writer in the first place called " flesh and blood," this he later called " corruption "; and what he had called the "kingdom of God," he now called "incorruption." But as to the body's substance itself, even then it will be flesh, just as the body of Christ is called flesh even after His Resurrection. Wherefore, too, the Apostle says: *It is sown a natural body, it shall rise a spiritual body;* [297] for then the harmony between the flesh and the spirit will be so perfect, the spirit quickening the subordinated flesh on which it is no longer dependent, that within our own selves there will be no conflicts any longer. As we shall then not have to cope with any enemy from without, so we shall not have to struggle within against our own selves.

92. But all those who, from among that mass of perdition [298] brought about by the first man, are not liberated by the *one Mediator of God and men,*[299] will indeed rise again, and each one with his own body, but only to be punished with the devil and his angels. However, whether these will rise again with all their physical defects and deformities, with the crippled and ill-shaped limbs that were theirs, what need is there of our concerning ourselves about this? Obviously, too, with their eternal damnation a certainty, the uncertainty of what happens to their physical appearance and beauty should not trouble us. Nor should we be disturbed by the problem of how theirs can be an incorruptible body if it can suffer, or a corruptible one if it cannot die. For there is no true life unless there is happy living; nor true incorruption unless there is well-being unscathed by any pain. But when an unhappy man is not permitted to die, then death itself, so to speak, dies not; and when perpetual pain never destroys but forever torments, corruption itself never ends. In Holy Scripture this is called the "second death." [300]

93. But neither the first death by which the soul is compelled to leave its body, nor the second by which the soul is not permitted to leave the body undergoing punishment, would have befallen man had no one sinned. The mildest punishment of all will of course be the lot of those who, apart from the original sin which they contracted, have added no further sin;[301] and as for the rest who have added such sins, the punishment of each will be the more bearable as his iniquity here was less grave.

CHAPTER 24

God's will to show mercy or judgment is always just and always efficacious.

94. Therefore, with the reprobate angels and men left to endure eternal punishment, the saints will understand more fully what blessings grace has bestowed upon them. Then the facts themselves will bring out more clearly what was meant by the words written in the Psalm: *Mercy and judgment I will sing unto thee, O Lord;*[302] for no one is redeemed except through unmerited mercy, and no one is condemned except through merited judgment.[303]

95. Then shall we understand what now eludes us. For example, when of two children one is to be taken up through mercy and the other to be left through judgment, and the one that is taken up will acknowledge what judgment would have been its due, had no mercy come to its assistance: why was the former taken up rather than the latter, when the cases of both were identically the same? Again, why were miracles[304] not wrought in the presence of men who, had this been done for them, would have done penance; whereas they were wrought in the presence of such as would not believe anyway? For indeed the Lord says most explicitly: *Woe to thee, Corozain, woe to thee, Bethsaida: for if in Tyre and Sidon had been wrought the miracles that have been wrought in you, they had long ago done penance in sackcloth and ashes.*[305] And surely, God did not act unjustly in not willing to save them, even though they could have been saved, had He so willed it.[306]

Then will be seen in the clearest light of wisdom what holy men now hold by faith in anticipation of grasping it by manifest understanding; namely, how certain and immutable and efficacious is the will of God; how many things He can do but does not will to do, though willing nothing which He cannot do; and how true is that which is sung in the Psalm: *But our God is in heaven above; He hath done all things in heaven and on earth, whatsoever He would.*[307] This certainly would not be true, if He had ever willed certain things and then failed to do them, or, what would be more degrading, if He had not done them because man's will prevented Him, the Omnipotent One, from carrying out His will.

Nothing, therefore, happens unless the Omnipotent wills it to happen: He either permits it to happen, or He brings it about Himself. **96.** Nor are we to doubt that God does well even when He permits evil.[308] For He does not permit this except for a just reason, and all that is just is indeed good. Although, therefore, what is evil, in so far as it is evil is not a good, nevertheless it is well that not only good but also evil should exist. For, were it not a good that evil things should also exist, the Omnipotent Good would most certainly not allow evil to be, since beyond doubt it is just as easy for Him not to allow what He does not will, as it is for Him to do what He wills. Unless we believe this, the very first sentence of our profession of faith is endangered, wherein we profess to believe in God the Father Almighty. For He is called Almighty for no other reason than that He can do whatever He wills, and because the effectiveness of His almighty will cannot be thwarted by the will of any creature whatsoever.[309]

97. Wherefore, we must look into the import of a statement concerning God—a statement put forth most truly by the Apostle: *Who will have all men to be saved.*[310] For, since not all men are saved—actually the great majority is not saved—it would indeed seem that what God wills does not happen, that as a matter of fact the will of God is thwarted by the will of man. And of course when there is question of the reason why all men are not saved, the usual answer is, because this is contrary to their own wills. But this cannot be said of children, who are not as yet capable of willing and not willing. For, were we to conclude that it should be charged to their will when in the course of being baptized they go through a baby's motions of protesting the performance with all their might, we would have to say that they are being saved even against their will. The Lord's language is a plainer one when in the Gospel He reproves the unholy city: *How often would I have gathered together thy children, as the hen her chickens, and thou wouldest not!*[311] This is as if the will of God had been overcome by the will of men, and as if the weaker by their unwillingness had made it impossible for the will of the stronger to be accomplished.[312] And where is that omnipotence by which *He hath done all things in heaven and on earth, whatsoever He would,*[313] if He willed to gather together the children of Jerusalem, and yet did not do it? Or is it not rather that Jerusalem did indeed not will that her children should be gathered together by Him, but that He, despite her opposition, gathered together those of her children whom He wanted? He did not simply will some things *in heaven and on earth* and accomplish them, while willing others without accomplishing them, but *He hath done all things, whatsoever He would.*

CHAPTER 25

God is free to show mercy to whom He wills.

98. Moreover, who would be so impious and foolish as to say that God cannot turn the evil wills of those He pleases, and when and where He pleases, towards good? And when He does this, He does so through mercy; when He does not, it is through justice; for, *He hath mercy on whom He will; and whom He will, He hardeneth.*[314] Now, when the Apostle said this, he was emphasizing divine grace. To illustrate this, he had previously spoken of those twins in the womb of Rebecca: *When these were not yet born, nor had done any good or evil, that the purpose of God according to election might stand, not of works but of Him that calleth, it was said to her: " The elder shall serve the younger."* [315] For the same reason the Apostles referred to another prophetic testimony, namely, this passage of the Scriptures: *I have loved Jacob, but I have hated Esau.*[316]

However, realizing how that which he had said might disturb those who by their understanding cannot reach these heights of grace, he says: *What shall we say then? Is there injustice with God? God forbid!* [317] For it does seem unfair that not on the basis of any merits of good or evil works God should love the one and hate the other.[318] Now, if he meant that the future good works of the one and the future evil works of the other—both certainly forseen [319] by God—should here be understood, he would never have said " not of works " but " of future works," and thus he would have solved the problem for us; rather, he would not have posited a problem to be solved. However, since the Apostle went on to say, *God forbid,* that is, God forbid that there should be injustice with God, he adds immediately, in order to prove that this happens through no injustice on the part of God: *For he saith to Moses: " I will have mercy on whom I will have mercy; and I will show mercy to whom I will be merciful."* [320] For who but a fool would consider God to be unfair either in inflicting penal justice upon the deserving or in showing mercy to the undeserving? He then draws the conclusion and says: *So then it is not of him that willeth, nor of him that runneth, but of God that showeth mercy.* [321] Hence, both the twins were born *by nature children of wrath,* [322] not indeed because of any works of their own, but because they were held in the fetters of damnation originally forged by Adam. But He who said, *I will have mercy on whom I will have mercy,* loved Jacob through mercy undeserved and held Esau in hatred through a judgment that was deserved. And since this judgment was the due of both, the one acknowledged in the presence of what happened to the other, that he was not to take any glory to himself for any merits marking him off from the other, merely because in his case, identical as it was with the other, he had not incurred the same penalty; but that he should glory in the richness of divine grace, for *it is not of him that willeth, nor of him that runneth, but of God that showeth mercy.* The whole appearance, and if I may say so, the very features of the Holy Scriptures are found to give this admonition by way of a most profound and salutary mystery to all who look in them intently—that *he that glorieth, let him glory in the Lord.* [328]

99. The Apostle, then, had set forth the mercy of God by saying: *So then it is not of him that willeth, nor of him that runneth, but of God that showeth mercy.* Next, purposing to speak also for His judgment—for the man who does not obtain mercy is not an object of unfairness but of judgment, there being no unfairness in God—he immediately added: *For the Scripture saith to Pharao: "To this purpose have I raised thee, that I may show my power in thee, and that my name may be declared throughout all the earth."* [324] He follows up these statements with a conclusion adapted to both, that is, His mercy and His justice, by saying: *Therefore He hath mercy on whom He will; and whom He will, He hardeneth.*[325] That is to say, He has mercy from out of His great goodness, and He hardens without showing any unfairness; so that neither he who is set free has cause to glory in any merits of his own, nor he who is condemned has reason to complain of anything but his own deserts. For it is grace alone that separates the redeemed from the lost, knowing that a condition brought upon them all by reason of their origin has joined them together [326] into one mass of perdition. But if any man on hearing this should say: *Why doth He then find fault? For who resisteth His will?* [327]—as if a man should not therefore be blamed for being evil, seeing that God *hath mercy on whom He will, and whom He will, He hardeneth*—God forbid that we should be ashamed to give the same answer as we know the Apostle gave: *O man, who art thou that replieth against God? Shall the thing formed say to Him that formed it: Why hast thou made me thus? Or hath not the potter power over the clay, of the same lump, to make one vessel unto honor, and another unto dishonor?* [328]

There are of course some stupid people who think that

in the present passage the Apostle was at a loss for an answer, and in his embarrassment for an explanation simply rebuked the presumption of the one contradicting him. But a weighty significance attaches to the words: *O man, who art thou?* And in problems such as these he does, it is true, bring a man back with a brief remark to the realization of his limited capacity, but at the same time he gives a profound explanation. For, if a man does not understand these matters, who is he that he should talk back to God? And if he does understand, then he finds nothing more to reply. Because if he understands, he realizes that the whole human race has been condemned in its rebellious head by a divine judgment so just, that even if not a single member of the race had been liberated, no man could have rightly censured the justice of God; [329] and he realizes too that it was but right that those who are liberated should be so liberated in order to show by contrast with the greater number of those not redeemed and left to a most just condemnation, what the entire human race deserved, and to what God's judgments, deserved by them as well, would bring them to, did not unmerited mercy come to their rescue, so that *every mouth* of those desiring to glory in their own merits *may be stopped*, and that *he that glorieth, may glory in the Lord.* [330]

CHAPTER 26

God always accomplishes His will, whether man co-operates with Him or whether he opposes Him.

100. These are *the great works of the Lord sought out according to all His wills.* [331] And so wisely are they sought out, that when His creatures, angels and man, had sinned, that is, had not done His will but their own, He still accomplished what He willed, and that through the same willfulness by which the opposite of the Creator's will was done. As the sovereign Good He turned to good account even what was evil, for the condemnation of those whom He has justly predestined to punishment,[332] and for the salvation of those whom He has mercifully predestined to grace. For, as far as they themselves were concerned, they did what God did not want done; but as regards God's omnipotence, they were in no way able to accomplish this. Yes, by the very fact that they acted against His will, His will concerning them was fulfilled. For the reason that *the works of the Lord are great, sought out according to all His wills,* lies in this, that in a wondrous, indescribable way even that which is done against His will is not done without His will. It simply could not be done if He did not permit it, and of course He permits it not against His will, but with it; nor would He in His goodness permit evil unless in His omnipotence He could bring good even out of evil.

101. Sometimes, however, a man with a good will desires something which God does not desire, and that too with a will that is also good—far more so and far more certainly so; for with Him an evil will is never possible. Take, for example, a good son desiring that his father continue to live, whereas it is God's will that he should die. Or again, it can happen that a man desires with an evil will what God in His good will likewise wills; for example, the case of a bad son desiring that his father should die, and God likewise willing it. Evidently, in the one instance the man desires what God does not want, while in the other he desires the same thing that God wills; still, the filial affection of the former, though he wills not what God wills, squares with God's will rather than does the impiety of the latter who does desire the same thing that God desires.

Such is the difference between what is proper for man and what is proper for God to will, and so much depends on what the purpose is towards which a person directs his will, whether it be acceptable or unacceptable. As a matter of fact, God brings about some of His purposes, which are of course good, through the evil designs of bad men; for example, it was by the good will of the Father working through the malevolence of the Jews that Christ was slain for us. And the result was so great a good that when the Apostle Peter protested that this should not take place, he was called Satan by Him who had come to be slain.[333] And how good seemed the intentions of the pious faithful who did not want the Apostle Paul to continue on to Jerusalem, lest he should there suffer the evils which the prophet Agabus had fore-told![334] And yet it was God's will that he should suffer them for the preaching of the faith of Christ, while also training the future martyr for Christ.[335] And this His good purpose He carried out not through the good intentions of the Christians, but through the evil ones of the Jews; and they who did not desire what He willed were more truly His than were the Jews through whose desires that was done which He willed. Both they and He brought about the same thing—He, through them, with a good purpose; they with their purpose evil.

102. But however strong the wills may be either of angels or of men—good or bad—and whether or not they will what God wills, the will of the Omnipotent is never defeated. Never can it be evil, because even when the will of God inflicts evil it is just; and what is just certainly is not evil. The omnipotent God, therefore, whether in commiseration

He hath mercy on whom He will, or in judgment *whom He will, He hardeneth*, does nothing unjustly, does nothing that He does not will, and does everything that He wills.

CHAPTER 27

St. Augustine interprets the text: God will have all men to be saved.

103. Therefore, when we hear and read in Sacred Scripture that He wills all men to be saved, although we know well that not all men are saved, we must not on that account depreciate in any way the most omnipotent will of God; rather, we must understand the words, *who will have all men to be saved*,[336] to mean that no man is saved unless God wills him to be saved, and not that there is no man whom He does not will to save, but that no one is saved unless He wills it; and that for this reason we should pray that He may will us to be saved, since if He wills it, this must come about. In fact, it was prayer to God that the Apostle was discussing when he made this statement.

It is in this sense, too, that we understand the expression in the Gospel, *which enlighteneth every man*:[337] not that there is no man who remains unenlightened, but that there is no man who is enlightened except by Him. At any rate, the import of the words, *who will have all men to be saved*, is not that there is no man whom He does not will to be saved, He who was unwilling to show forth the power of His miracles before those who, He said, would have done penance had He done so; but by " all men " we should understand every single class and group into which mankind is differentiated—kings and private persons, nobles and com-

moners, the high, the low, the learned, the ignorant; the
healthy, the sick, the bright, the dull, the simple; the rich,
the poor, the middle class; males, females, infants, children,
the growing youth, young men and women, the middle-aged,
the old; people of every tongue and custom, of all arts and
professions; people of a countless variety of wills and minds
and whatever else distinguishes men. For, from which of these
groups does not God will that some men should be saved in
all nations through His only-begotten Son our Lord, and,
therefore, does save them, knowing as we do that the Omnipotent cannot will in vain whatever He may will? For the
Apostle had enjoined that prayers should be said for *all* men,
and had added specifically: *for kings and for all that are in
high station*,[338] men who might be thought in their worldly
pomp and pride to shrink from the lowliness of the Christian
faith. Continuing, he said: *For this is good and acceptable
in the sight of God our Saviour*,[339] that is, that prayers should
be offered also for such as these; and, to remove any ground
for despair, he added immediately: *Who will have all men
to be saved and to come to the knowledge of the truth*.[340]
Yes, truly, God has deemed it good that to the prayers of the
lowly He should deign to grant the salvation of the exalted;
and assuredly we see that it so happens.

The Lord likewise used this manner of speech in the
Gospels when He said to the Pharisees: *You tithe mint and
rue and every herb*.[341] The Pharisees of course did not pay
tithes on what belonged to others, nor on all the herbs of all
peoples through all lands. Therefore, understanding " every
herb " to mean " every kind of herb," so in that other passage we may understand " all men " to signify " all classes
of men." Any other interpretation is acceptable too, as long
as we are not forced to believe that anything which the

Omnipotent willed to be done was not done. For if—and here there can be no ambiguity whatever—*He hath done all things in heaven and on earth, whatsoever He pleased,*[342] as Truth sings of Him, He certainly did not will to do anything that He has not done.

CHAPTER 28

God's will concerning man before and after the Fall. God redeems man through Christ the Mediator and gives him heaven as a reward for his fidelity to grace.

104. Wherefore, too, God would have willed to preserve the first man in that state of well-being in which he had been created, and in due time after the birth of his children bring him to better things without the intervention of death, where not only would he have been incapable of sin, but free from even the desire of sinning; I say, He would have willed this, had He foreknown that man would have an abiding will to remain sinless as he had been made. But since He foresaw that man would misuse his free will, that is, that he would commit sin, God rather predetermined His will in such a way that He Himself would do good through him doing evil, and thus the good will of the Omnipotent would not be rendered void by the evil will of man, but would be fulfilled in spite of it.

105. Thus it was indeed reasonable that man should at the beginning be so constituted as to be able to will either good or evil; not without reward if he chose the good, and not without punishment if he chose the evil. But in his afterlife he will be so constituted as not to be able to desire evil. But this does not mean that he will lack free will. In fact, his will will be much more free because it will be utterly impossible for him to serve sin. And certainly neither should fault be found with a will, nor does it cease to be will, nor should its freedom be denied, by which we so desire to be happy that not only do we not wish to be unhappy, but find it utterly impossible to have such a desire at all.[343] As, therefore, it is characteristic of our soul even now not to desire unhappiness, so, too, in the life to come it will forever be characterized by its aversion to evil. But such an arrangement should not be taken lightly, one by which God wished to show how good the rational creature is that is able to choose not to sin, though that one which cannot sin at all, is better. So, too, it was an inferior form of immortality— but immortality it was—by which man was also able to avoid death; though the immortality of the life to come is of a higher order, one in which it is impossible for man to die.[344]

106. The former immortality was lost to humanity through the exercise of free will; the latter it will obtain through grace, though it was to obtain it through merit had it not sinned. But even then there could have been no merit without grace; because even though sin came about in free will alone, nevertheless free will would not have sufficed to preserve innocence, unless through participation in the immutable Good divine assistance had been offered. Thus, for example, it is within man's power to die when he wants to, since any man can, by simply abstaining from food—not to mention other means—do away with himself. But the mere will to maintain life is not enough, if the helps of food or any other preservatives of life are lacking.

So, too, in Paradise man was able to destroy himself by forsaking the cause of right through the agency of his will;

but if his life of innocence was to be preserved, his mere will to preserve it would have been insufficient, did not God who had made him come to his aid. But since the Fall the mercy of God is even greater, because free will itself needs to be freed from the bondage of which the masters are sin and death. And it is out of the question for free will to realize this freedom through its own power; this it can do only through the grace of God, rooted in the faith of Christ. And so the will itself, as Scripture puts it, *is made ready beforehand by the Lord* for the reception of the other gifts of God through which we come into possession of His Gift everlasting.[345]

107. Hence, even eternal life itself, which is surely the reward of good works, is called by the Apostle a gift of God. *For the wages of sin*, he says, *is death. But the grace of God, life everlasting, in Christ Jesus our Lord.*[346] Wages[347] for military service are paid as something due, and not given as a donation. Therefore he said, *the wages of sin is death*, to show that death was inflicted not undeservedly but as something due to sin. But a gift is not a gift at all, if it is not made gratuitously. Consequently, we are to understand that even man's good deserts are themselves gifts of God. When, therefore, eternal life is bestowed because of them, what else is this but a return of grace for grace?[348]

Man, therefore, was made righteous in such wise, that he could persevere in righteousness with divine assistance, though he could by his own free will depart from it. Whichever course he might choose, in either case God's will would have been done, either by man complying with it, or at least by God concerning him. Accordingly, since he preferred to do his own will rather than God's, the will of God was fulfilled concerning him; for out of one and the same mass of perdition which issued from his stock, God makes *one vessel unto honor, another unto dishonor;* [349] unto honor through His mercy, unto dishonor through His judgment. No one is to glory in man, and, consequently, not in himself.[350]

108. For certainly we would not be redeemed even by the *one Mediator of God and men, the man Jesus Christ,*[351] if He were not also God. Now, when Adam was created—a righteous man to be sure—there was no need of a mediator.[352] But once sin had created a wide rift between the human race and God, it was necessary that a mediator, who alone was born and lived and was put to death without sin, should reconcile us with God even to the extent of obtaining for us the resurrection of the body unto life everlasting, in order that the pride of man might be rebuked and cured through the humility of God; [353] that man might be made to see how far he had departed from God, when the Incarnate God came to summon him back; that man in his stubbornness might receive an example of obedience from the God-Man; [354] that the fountain of grace might be opened by the Only-Begotten taking the form of a servant, a form which had no antecedent merits; that the resurrection also of the body, promised to the redeemed, might be presaged in the Resurrection of the Redeemer; that the devil might be conquered by that same nature which he rejoiced to have deceived, without man, however, taking glory in himself, lest pride spring up anew. And to this add whatever else those who are proficient in these matters can perceive and explain, or perceive without being able to explain, concerning the great mystery of the Mediator.[355]

CHAPTER 29

Purgatory, heaven, hell. The City of God and the City of Satan.

109. During the time, however, which intervenes between man's death and the final resurrection, the souls remain in places specially reserved for them, according as each is deserving of rest or tribulation for the disposition he has made of his life in the flesh.[356]

110. And it cannot be denied that the souls of the dead obtain relief through the piety of their living friends, when they have the Sacrifice of the Mediator offered for them,[357] or when alms [358] are given in the Church on their behalf. But these things benefit those only who during their lives merited that these services should one day help them. For there is a manner of life neither so good as not to need such helps after death, nor so bad that they cannot be of benefit.[359] But there is likewise the man so entirely devoted to good that he does not need these helps; and, again, one so steeped in evil that when he departs this life even these helps avail him nothing. Evidently, then, it is in this life that the basis is laid on which a person deserves to have his condition in the afterlife alleviated or aggravated; and, therefore, let no one hope that what he neglected to do here he will merit with God when he dies.

Nor does it follow that the constant practice of the Church thus to intercede for the dead [360] is opposed to that statement of the Apostle which reads: *For we must all stand before the judgment seat of Christ, that every one may receive according to what he has done through the body, whether it be good or evil;* [361] for that very merit whereby these services which I have mentioned can benefit a man, is acquired by each one for himself during his life in the body.[362] Certainly not all can benefit by such services. And why do not all derive benefit from them, if not because of the differences that mark each person's life in the body? When, therefore, sacrifices either of the altar or of alms of any kind are offered for all the baptized dead, they are thank offerings for the very good; for those who were not very bad they are propitiatory offerings; and, though for the very bad they have no significance as helps for the dead, they do bring a measure of consolation to the living. And those who actually receive such profit, receive it in the form either of a complete remission of sin, or of at least an amelioration of their sentence.[363]

111. But after the resurrection, when the general judgment has been held and concluded, there will remain two cities,[364] each with its own boundaries—the one Christ's, the other the devil's; the one embracing the good, the other, the bad, with both consisting of angels and men. For the one group the will to sin will be impossible, for the other, the power to do so. Nor will any manner of death remain. The former will live truly and happily in eternal life, the latter will drag on, miserable in eternal death—unable to die; for both are now without end. But among the former some will outrank others in bliss, and among the latter some will have a more bearable portion of misery than others.

112. It is in vain, therefore, that some, indeed, very many, out of mere human sentiment deplore the eternal punishment and the unceasing and everlasting torments of the damned, and do not believe that such things will be. True, they take their stand not by arguing against the Divine

Scriptures, but, governed by their feelings, they tone down everything that seems harsh and give a milder turn to the meaning of what they try to believe was said more to terrify than to express literal truth; for *God*, they quote, *will not forget to show mercy, nor will He in His anger shut up His mercies.*[365] Yes, such is the text in a holy psalm. But without the least doubt this is to be understood of those persons who are called *vessels of mercy,*[366] because even with them it is not on account of any merits of their own, but through God's commiseration that they are freed from misery.[367] Or, if these people think that the passage applies to all men, it does not follow that they must therefore suppose that the punishment of those can cease of whom it is said: *And these shall go into everlasting punishment.*[368] Otherwise it might be thought that the happiness of those concerning whom the contrary is said, *But the just, into life everlasting,*[369] will some day also come to an end.

But let them believe, if they care to, that the torments of the damned are to some extent mitigated at certain intervals.[370] Even so, the wrath of God, that is, their condemnation— for it is this, and not some emotional disturbance in the divine mind which is called the wrath of God—can still be understood to rest upon them. Thus, even in His wrath, that is, while His wrath endures, He would not withhold His mercies; yet, not so as to put an end to their eternal punishment, but rather to apply or to interpose some little respite from their torments. For the Psalm does not say " to end His wrath " or " after His wrath has passed," but *in His wrath*. If this wrath were all, and were it present in the smallest imaginable degree: to lose the kingdom of God, to be an exile from the city of God, to be a stranger to the life of God, to want for the great abundance of God's sweetness which He has hidden for those who fear Him but made ready for those who hope in Him [371]—this would be a punishment so great that, given that it is eternal, no torments known to us could be compared with it, no matter through how many ages they might extend.

113. The perpetual death, then, of the damned, that is, their separation from the life of God, will go on without end [372] and will be their common lot, regardless of what people, prompted by human sentiments, may conjure up about different kinds of punishment or a mitigation or interruption of their torments. Likewise, the life of the saints will continue forever and be shared by all, no matter what distinctions of rank may obtain in the glory of their harmonious splendor.[373]

CHAPTER 30

All that pertains to the virtue of Hope is summed up in the Lord's Prayer.

114. From this confession of faith, which is briefly summed up in the Creed, and which to carnal thought is milk for babes, but to spiritual reflection and study is meat for strong men,[374] is born the good hope of the faithful, with holy charity as its companion. But of all the matters which are to be believed in the true spirit of faith, only those pertain to hope which are contained in the Lord's Prayer. For, *cursed be every one*, so the Holy Scriptures testify, *that placeth his hope in man.*[375] It follows that one who puts his hope in himself is likewise held by the bond of this curse. We should, therefore, beg of the Lord alone for whatsoever we may hope to accomplish ourselves in the way of good works, or hope to obtain as a reward for good deeds done.

115. Wherefore, according to the Evangelist Matthew the Lord's Prayer appears to contain seven petitions, three of which request eternal goods, the remaining four, temporal goods necessary for the attainment of the eternal. For, when we say: *Hallowed be Thy name, Thy kingdom come, Thy will be done on earth as it is in heaven* [376] (which latter words some have with good reason interpreted to mean " in body and in spirit "), these are things to be retained forever. They are begun here; they are increased in us as we make progress; and in their perfection, a state to be hoped for in the other life, they will be an everlasting possession. But when we say: *Give us this day our daily bread, and forgive us our debts, as we also forgive our debtors, and bring us not into temptation, but deliver us from evil,* [377] who does not see that these things pertain to the necessaries of this life? In that eternal life, therefore, where we hope to be forever, the hallowing of God's name, His kingdom, and His will will abide in everlasting perfection in our souls and bodies. The bread is called " daily bread " for the reason that here below this is a necessity, and that to the extent required by soul and body, whether the term is understood in a spiritual or a physical sense, or in both senses. Here, too, where there is commission of sins, is the place for the remission which we ask. Here are the temptations which allure or urge us to sin. And, lastly, here is the evil from which we pray to be freed. But in that other world none of these things exist.

116. Now, with the Evangelist Luke the Lord's Prayer embraces not seven, but five petitions. [378] But of course this does not mean that he disagreed with the other version;

rather, by his very brevity he has shown how the seven petitions should be understood. For God's name is hallowed in
the spirit; and God's kingdom will come in the resurrection
of the flesh. Luke, therefore, by showing that the third
petition is to some extent a repetition of the first two, helps us
to a better understanding of it by omitting it. He then goes
on to state three further petitions: concerning the daily bread,
the remission of sins, and the avoidance of temptation. However, what Matthew put in the last place, " but deliver us
from evil," Luke omitted, to make us see that it belongs to
what was previously said about temptation. In fact, this is
why Matthew said " *but* deliver us," not " *and* deliver us," to
make clear that we have here practically only one petition:
do not this, but this. Thus everyone would know that he is
delivered from evil by the fact that he is not led into
temptation.

CHAPTER 31

*Charity is the crown of all the virtues. The four states of
man.*

117. And now, as to charity, which the Apostle said is
greater than the other two, that is, than faith and hope,[379]
the more there is of it, the better is the man in whom it
dwells.[380] When the question is asked whether a man is
good, one is not interested in what he believes or what are
his hopes, but only what he loves. For beyond any doubt, a
man with a right love also has the right faith and hope. But
one who has no love, believes in vain, even though what he
believes may be the truth. And he hopes in vain, even
though the object of his hope theoretically is a part of true
happiness—unless this is also part of what he believes and

hopes, namely, that in answer to his prayer he may receive
the gift of love. For, true as it may be that he cannot hope
without love, yet it is possible that he does not love the means
without which he cannot realize the object of his hope. For
example, a man might hope for eternal life—and who is there
that does not love it?—and not love justice, without which
no one obtains eternal life. And as to the true faith of Christ,
it is that which the Apostle praises, faith *that worketh by
charity*;[381] and what its love does not yet embrace, it asks
that it may receive it, seeks that it may find, and knocks that
it may be opened to it.[382] It is this faith that obtains what
the law ordains.[383] For without the Gift of God, that is, without the Holy Spirit, through whom charity is diffused in our
hearts, the law can command, but cannot help; and besides,
it can make a man a transgressor, since he cannot excuse
himself on the plea of ignorance. Plainly, carnal lust reigns
where the charity of God is absent.

118. Life lived according to the flesh, in the darkest
abysses of ignorance, with no restraint imposed by reason—
this is man's first state.[384] Then, when *by the law the knowledge of sin*[385] comes to him, and the Holy Spirit is as yet
not present with His assistance, he is, though striving to live
according to the law, overcome and knowingly sins, thus
becoming a subject and slave of sin; *for by whom a man is
overcome, to the same also is he bound as slave.*[386] Such is
the effect produced by the knowledge of the commandment,
that sin works in man all manner of concupiscence[387] in
addition to the guilt of the first fall,[388] and thus there is fulfilled what is written: *The law entered in, that sin might
abound.*[389] This is the second state of man. But if God looks
upon him, and he then believes that God helps him to carry
out His commands and begins to be moved by the Spirit of

God,[390] then, with charity the dominant force in him, his desires run counter to the flesh; [391] and, although there is still in him some opposition arising from his own nature as yet not entirely cured of its infirmity, nevertheless he lives as a just man by faith,[392] and he lives justified in so far as he does not yield to evil lust but overcomes it by his love of holiness. This is the third state—that of the man of good hope. And for one who advances in this state with holy perseverance, there is in store peace at last, which is consummated after this life in the repose of the spirit and afterwards also in the resurrection of the body.

Of these four different states of man the first is before the law, the second under the law, the third under grace, and the fourth in full and perfect peace. So, too, the fortunes of God's people followed set periods of time according to His good pleasure, who *ordereth all things in measure, and number, and weight.*[393] First, His people existed before the law; then, under the law which was given by Moses; next, under grace revealed in the first advent of the Mediator. This grace had not previously been wanting to those who were to be given it, though in the temporal economy it was veiled and hidden. For evidently no one among the just men of old could find salvation apart from the faith of Christ. And, unless He had been known also to them, the prophecies— now plain, now obscure—which their ministry served to give us concerning Him, could not have been made.

119. And in whatever of these four, let us say, ages, the grace of regeneration finds a person, all his past sins are then and there forgiven him, and the guilt which ·he contracted at birth is taken away by his second birth. And so true is it that *the Spirit breatheth where He will,*[394] that some men never experience the second state, that of servitude under the law, but with the law begin to receive divine assistance.

120. However, before a man can receive the law, he must have life according to the flesh. But once he has received the sacrament of regeneration, no harm will come to him should he depart from this life at once; [395] *for to this end Christ died and rose again, that He might be Lord both of the living and of the dead.*[396] Nor will the realm of death retain him for whom He suffered death who is *free among the dead.*[397]

CHAPTER 32

The whole law depends on charity, for God is charity.

121. Accordingly, all the divine commandments hark back to charity, concerning which the Apostle says: *Now the end of the commandment is charity, from a pure heart, and a good conscience, and an unfeigned faith.*[398] Every commandment therefore has for its end charity, that is, it is charity that determines every commandment. But whatever is done either through fear of punishment or from some carnal motive so as not to be determined by that charity which the Holy Spirit diffuses in our hearts,[399] is not done as it ought to be done, all appearances notwithstanding. And of course the charity meant here is the love of God and the love of our neighbor, and truly *on these two commandments dependeth the whole law and the prophets.*[400] Here add the Gospel, too, and the Apostles; for it is in these alone that we hear the saying: *The end of the commandment is charity,* and again: *God is love.*[401] Hence, all of God's commandments, one of which is: *Thou shalt not commit adultery,*[402] and whatsoever, though not commanded, is recommended by way of spiritual counsel, an example of which is: *It is good for a man not to touch a woman* [403]—all these things are carried

out in the right manner when they are motivated by love for
God, and because of God, for our neighbor.[404]

All this holds true of the world we are in and the world to
come. Now we love God through faith; then, through
sight.[405] Here we love even our neighbor through faith, for
we who are ourselves mortal do not know the hearts of mortal
men. But in the world to come the Lord *will bring to light
the hidden things of darkness, and will make manifest the
thoughts of the heart; and then shall every man have praise
from God.*[406] For each man will praise and love in his fellow
man that which God Himself, not wanting it to remain
unknown, will bring to light. And passion wanes as love
waxes strong, the latter ascending to heights than which
there are no greater; for *greater love no man hath than that
a man lay down his life for his friends.*[407] Who, then, can
fathom how great love will be in the world to come, where
there will be no passion for it to overcome or even to re-
strain? For when death's claims will be no more, the perfection of self-possession will obtain.

CHAPTER 33

Conclusion.

122. But it is time that we should reach the end of this
book. Judge for yourself whether you should call it a
handbook, or should use it as such. As for myself, thinking
as I did that your zeal in Christ should not be esteemed
lightly, and believing and hoping good things of you in the
help of our Redeemer, and loving you deeply as one of His
members, I have to the best of my ability written this book
for you on faith, hope and charity. May its usefulness be
equal to its length!

NOTES

INTRODUCTION

[1] From the Greek ἐγχειρίδιον — the late Latin *manuale* = a manual, handbook, or vademecum. The word had been used in Latin before Augustine. In the second century the Roman jurist Sextus Pomponius wrote a *Liber singularis enchiridii*. Of this a long passage survives by having been incorporated in the *Digesta* of Justinian (1. 2. 2). Cf. H. F. Jolowicz, *Historical Introduction to the Study of Roman Law* (Cambridge 1932) 391. St. Jerome (in the Jeromian compilation, *Breviarium in Psalmos, prol.* [ML 26.821D]) mentions "Origenis psalterium, quod *Enchiridion* ille vocabat." See also *Thes. ling. Lat.* 5 *s. v.*

[2] In one of his letters to Count Darius (*Ep.* 231. 7) he speaks of the treatise as a *liber grandis.*

[3] Augustine also mentions the title in a letter to Darius, *loc. cit.*, and in *De octo Dulcitii quaest.* 1.10: In eo *libro cui titulus est de fide, spe, et caritate,* quem scripsi ad . . . Laurentium . . . See also Possidius, *Indiculus* 6.

[4] *De fide et symbolo; De agone Christiano.*

[5] Cf., e. g., F. Kattenbusch, *Das apostolische Symbol* 2 (Leipzig 1900) 403 f.

[6] Cf. F. Abert, *Sancti Thomae Aquinatis compendium theologiae* (Würzburg 1896) 17; P. Simon, *Das Handbüchlein des hl. Augustinus* (Dokumente der Religion 1, Paderborn 1923) 6 f.

[7] See Kattenbusch, *op. cit.* 2. 409.

[8] A. Harnack, *History of Dogma* 5 (trans. by N. Buchanan, Boston 1902) 217 ff. The disparate treatment of the subjects announced for discussion in the title, *De fide, spe et caritate,* and the consequent problem of a proper division of the entire treatise is discussed by J. Rivière, "Comment diviser l'Enchiridion de S. Augustin," *Bull. de litt. ecclés.* 43 (1942) 99-115.

[9] Rom. 11. 32.

[10] *Op. cit.* 177 f.

[11] Cf. *The Imitation of Christ,* ed. by E. J. Klein (New York 1941) 113.

[12] ML 40. 229.

[13] Cf. O. Scheel, *Augustins Enchiridion* (Samml. ausgew. kirchen- und dogmengesch. Quellenschriften, 2. Reihe, 4: 2nd ed., Tübingen 1930) iv.

THE TREATISE

[1] For St. Augustine the final purpose of all learning is the acquisition of happiness in God. *Nulla est homini causa philosophandi, nisi ut beatus sit*, he says in *De civ. Dei* 19. 13. Concerning this aspect of Augustinian thought, see M. E. Baudin, " Le pragmatisme religieux de Pascal," *Rev. des sciences rel.* 5 (1925) 61 ff.

[2] 1 Cor. 1. 20; cf. Isa. 19. 12 and 33. 18.

[3] Wisd. 6. 26.

[4] Rom. 16. 19. The sentence which follows is not found in the older manuscripts and is considered spurious. The Scriptural passage contained in it is from Eccli. 1. 1.

[5] Job 28. 28: *pietas* est sapientia. Note here the interesting divergence of Augustine's text from the Vulgate. The latter has: *timor Domini*, ipsa est sapientia (" the *fear of the Lord*, that is wisdom "). However, in Jerome's first revision of the Latin text of the Old Testament, which he undertook in the year 386 and based on the Septuagint version, this passage in Job also reads: *pietas* est sapientia (cf. ML 29. 95A). Augustine's translation of θεοσέβεια of the Septuagint with *pietas* (" filial reverence ") and his interpretation of it as *cultus Dei* (" worship of God ") are expressed again in the close parallel in *Serm.* 16. 2 Denis (76 Morin): Et ecce, quoniam dixit homini ipsa sapientia, " Ecce, *pietas est sapientia* "; *ad sapientiam vero hominis pertinet colere Deum.* . . .

[6] Augustine insists frequently on the twofold source of knowledge: reason and faith, or reason and revelation. In his *Cont. Acad.* 3. 43 he says: Nulli dubium est genuino pondere nos impelli ad discendum, *auctoritatis atque rationis.*

[7] Gal. 5. 6.

[8] *Species* = beatific vision; cf. Augustine, *De Trin.* 14. 2: *Species, qua videantur quae credebantur*; also *De cat. rud.* 25. 47, and J. P. Christopher's observations, ACW 2 (1946) 143 n. 302.

[9] 1 Cor. 3. 11.

[10] Unlike the philosophical schools, *the City of God*, according to the Bishop of Hippo, does not allow diverse and contradictory views to be held or freely debated by its members. Those who profess doctrines alien to those taught by Mother Church become by that very fact heretics, and are looked upon as her enemies. Cf. *De civ. Dei.* 18.51. This conception of the Church as the guardian

of orthodoxy undoubtedly implies a belief in her *infallibility*. A. Harnack, *History of Dogma* 5 (trans. by N. Buchanan, Boston 1902) 77, says: " Having forced his way through scepticism to the truth of the Catholic Church, he regarded the latter as the rock on which his faith was founded." Cf. *ibid*. 150.

[11] Joel 2. 32.

[12] Rom. 10. 14.

[13] The Creed and the Lord's Prayer played a very important role in the catechumenate. In the solemn ceremonies of the *traditio* and *redditio symboli* and the *traditio* and *redditio orationis dominicae* they were delivered to the catechumens to be learned by heart. Cf. W. Roetzer, *Des hl. Augustinus Schriften als liturgiegeschichtliche Quelle* (Munich 1930); J. Quasten, *Monumenta Eucharistica et liturgica vetustissima* (Bonn 1935-37) 103 ff., 167 ff., 325.

[14] Lucan, *Phars.* 2. 15.

[15] Vergil, *Aen.* 4. 419. But here modern commentators of Vergil quite correctly interpret the word *sperare* differently: Dido speaks of " foreseeing," " anticipating " her great woe, not of " hoping " for it. One of the grammarians referred to in the following was Servius who wrote his commentary on Vergil probably between the years 395-410 — only about a dozen years before Augustine wrote the *Enchiridion*. For his observations on the present verse, see G. Thilo–H. Hagen, *Servii Grammatici in Vergilii carmina commentarii* 1 (1891) 539 f. Cf. also the *Codex Bernensis* 16 in H. Hagen, *Anecdota Helvetica* (Leipzig 1870) xlv. 26.

[16] Heb. 11. 1. St. Augustine accepted the Epistle to the Hebrews as canonical. Cf. *De doctr. Christ.* 2. 8. 13, where he speaks of *fourteen* Pauline epistles; also *De pecc. mer. et remiss.* 1. 50: *Ad Hebraeos . . . epistola quamquam nonnullis incerta sit, . . . magis . . . me movet auctoritas ecclesiarum orientalium, quae hanc etiam in canonicis habent*. However, Augustine remained uncertain in regard to the Pauline authorship of the epistle (cf. *De civ. Dei.* 16. 22). See F. Prat, *La théologie de Saint Paul* 1 (18th ed.; Paris 1930) 555.

[17] Here the words *sacra eloquia* (= " holy pronouncements," sacred eloquence ") are used. For St. Augustine and for others among the Fathers this was a favored designation for the Scriptures. See J. P. Christopher's note, ACW 2 (1946) 112 f.

[18] It is interesting to note that on this question, which remains still the object of theological controversy, Augustine was satisfied merely to express his preference without charging others with error.

[19] Rom. 8. 24 f.

[20] James 2. 19.

[21] Gal. 5. 6.

[22] St. Augustine expresses this same thought in *Ep.* 120. 8: *Pia fides sine spe et sine caritate esse non vult.* He is here describing a just man, in whom the virtues of faith, hope, and charity actually abide. See S. Harent: " Espérance," *Dict. de theol. cath.* 5 (Paris 1913) 607. For a brilliant, though lengthy, discussion of this passage, read J. B. Faure, *Enchiridion de fide, spe et caritate S. Aurelii Augustini* (Naples 1847) 20 ff.

[23] *Physici.* This probably refers to the philosophers of the Early Ionian School, such as Thales, Anaximander, and Anaximenes; men who were students of nature and who devoted themselves to the inquiry into the origin of the physical universe. As such, they would be distinguished from the Pythagorean School, whose followers were more directly interested in the number theory, to which Augustine alludes in the passage which follows.

[24] Augustine constantly proclaims the insufficiency of philosophy as a sure guide to the good and the true. He insists over and over again on the need of supernatural strength to free the will from the chains of the flesh and of supernatural light to banish from the mind the darkness of skepticism. Cf. E. Gilson, *Introduction à l'étude de Saint Augustin* (Etudes de phil. méd. 11, 2nd ed., Paris 1943) 299 ff.

[25] Few men in the history of Christianity have written so much or so well on the Blessed Trinity as did the saintly Bishop of Hippo. Yet he did not hesitate to confess his ignorance in these immortal lines: *Tamen cum quaeritur quid tres, magna prorsus inopia humanum laborat eloquium. Dictum est tamen: tres personae, non ut illud diceretur, sed ne taceretur.* Cf. *De Trin.* 5. 9. 10. See other texts and references in J. Martin, *Saint Augustin* (2nd ed., Paris 1923) 121 n. 4.

[26] Cf. Gen. 1. 31. This entire paragraph is of course directed against the Manichaeans whose disciple Augustine had been for nine long years of his early manhood, and against whom he had written numerous treatises two or three decades before he wrote his *Enchiridion.* According to this sect, all evil, physical and moral, owes its origin to an essentially evil principle, existing from all eternity together with an essentially good principle. For their teachings, cf. P. Alfaric, *Les écritures manichéennes* (2 vols., Paris 1918-19).

[27] Vergil, *Aen.* 10. 100: *Rerum cui summa potestas* (trans. by J. W. Mackail). For a careful study of Vergil's influence on St. Augustine, see K. H. Schelkle, *Vergil in der Deutung Augustins* (Stuttgart 1939).

[28] Concerning the incompatibility of evil with the nature of God, cf. E. F. Micka, *The Problem of Divine Anger in Arnobius and Lactantius* (Stud. in Christ. Ant. 4, Washington 1943) 64 ff., 94 ff.

[29] In his *Confessions*, 7. 11, St. Augustine states that for a long time he could not explain the origin of evil: *Quaerebam unde malum, et non erat exitus.* But once he had received from the philosophy of the Neo-Platonists the idea that being and good are interchangeable, and that evil therefore cannot be a positive entity but only the privation of some good, he had found a solution to the problem of evil from which he never again departed. Cf. the reflections by P. Simon, *Das Handbüchlein des hl. Augustinus* (Paderborn 1923) 139 ff.

[30] It is only through the destructive force of corruption that we understand clearly how exalted a good the essence of an incorruptible soul really is.

[31] Isa. 5. 20.

[32] Matt. 12. 35.

[33] These words are like an anticipation of the doctrine laid down many centuries later by the Church in the Fourth Lateran Council, that all things, even the devil himself, are good so far as they come from the creative act of God, and that if they become evil it is through the corruption of the good. Cf. H. Denziger — C. Bannwart — J. B. Umberg, *Enchiridion symbolorum, definitionum et declarationum* (21-23rd ed., Freiburg i. Br. 1937) no. 428.

[34] Matt. 7. 18.

[35] Cf. Matt. 7. 16.

[36] Matt. 12. 33.

[37] Vergil, *Georg.* 2. 490 (trans. by J. W. Mackail).

[38] Vergil, *Georg.* 2. 479 f. (trans. by T. C. Williams). It would be a real mistake to deduce from such statements as these that Augustine had come to hold secular knowledge in contempt, and that the Christianity of his time was hostile to science. For a good discussion of this problem, see W. R. Halliday, *The Pagan Background of Early Christianity* (London 1925) 171 f.

[39] For the relations of St. Augustine with Donatism, see P. Monceaux, *Histoire littéraire de l'Afrique chrétienne* 7: *Saint Augustin et le donatisme* (Paris 1923).

[40] The incident is also recorded by Augustine's biographer, Possidius, *Vita Aug.* 12. Among the Donatist schismatics there were armed bands of ruffians known as *Circumcelliones.* Possidius, himself the bishop of Calama in Numidia, was not so fortunate in escaping their terrorism. Sent on a special mission by St. Augustine, he was waylaid. He managed to escape, only to be almost cremated when his pursuers set fire to the house in which he had taken refuge. See Augustine's report, *Ep.* 105. 4; also *Cont. Crescon.* 3. 50.

[41] Vergil, *Ecl.* 8. 42.

[42] Matt. 5. 37.

[43] Cf. Apoc. 21. 27.

[44] Saint Augustine wrote two works on the subject: *De mendacio,* written about the year 395, and *Contra mendacium ad Consentium,* written a year or so before the *Enchiridion.* It is quite certain that it is the second of these two works which is referred to in this passage. It is approximately one-half as long as the *Enchiridion,* and gives Augustine's definitive teaching on lying.

[45] The treatise *Contra mendacium,* was written, as Augustine himself tells us (*Retract.* 2. 60), to set aright those over-zealous Catholics who did not find it reprehensible to deny their faith and to simulate Priscillianism in order to ferret out who were the real followers of this heresy. The Priscillianists erred, for example, regarding the Trinity and the humanity of Christ; hence, as Augustine says, to find them out some Catholics were ready " to speak falsely . . . about the nature of God Himself."

[46] A familiar quotation from Sallust, *Cat.* 10. 5: aliud clausum in pectore, aliud in lingua promptum habere.

[47] Isa. 5. 20.

[48] Cf. F. J. Dölger, " Die Sünde in Blindheit und Unwissenheit," *Ant. u. Christ.* 2 (1930) 222-29. See also the interesting study by B. Roland-Gosselin, " Erreur et péché," *Rev. de phil.* 28 (1928) 466-78.

[49] Cf. Acts 12. 9.

[50] Vergil, *Aen.* 10. 392.

[51] The *Contra Academicos* was written by St. Augustine in November, 386, in the company of his friends at Cassiciacum. His decision to become a Christian had already been made. In writing the treatise he freed himself from the last shackles of his errant thinking — skepticism. For a brief exposition of the three dialogues constituting the work and the circumstances of its composition, cf.

V. J. Bourke, *Augustine's Quest of Wisdom* (Milwaukee 1945) 72-74.

[52] Rom. 1. 17; cf. also Hab. 2. 4, Gal. 3. 11, Heb. 10. 38. This text has been used frequently in an attempt to prove that St. Paul accepted the faith by which we are saved in the sense of confidence in Christ's merits. Augustine has been charged with the same belief. But the Bishop of Hippo, using this very text of the Apostle, insists very emphatically and states very clearly that faith as an assent of the mind to truths revealed by God is a necessary condition for salvation.

[53] For the history of this distinction, cf. O. Lottin, "La nature du péché d'ignorance," *Rev. Thomiste* 15 (1932) 1-35.

[54] Gal. 5. 6; cf. also 2 Cor. 5. 7.

[55] Cf. Gen. 37. 33.

[56] Cf. Rom. 8. 20 ff.; Eccle. 1. 2; 2. 26.

[57] Compare this unequivocal condemnation of every lie with the antecedent attitude. Plato, for example, permits statesmen to lie in behalf of the common good (cf. *Rep.* 389 b). Even great Christian writers prior to Augustine — Origen, St. Hilary, St. John Chrysostum — could allow the telling of a falsehood under certain conditions. Cf. J. Mausbach, *Catholic Moral Teaching and its Antagonists* (6th ed. trans. by A. M. Buchanan, New York 1914) 113 f.; L. Godefroy, "Mensonge," *Dict. de théol. Cat.* 10. 1 (1928) 555-69; A. Reul, *Die sittlichen Ideale des heiligen Augustinus* (Paderborn 1928) 110-15. For the influence of the present passage on the doctrine of early Scholasticism, cf. A. Landgraf, "Definition und Sündhaftigkeit der Lüge nach der Lehre der Frühscholastik," *Zeitschr. f. kath. Theol.* 62 (1939) 50-85, 157-80.

[58] Matt. 5. 37.

[59] Matt. 6. 12.

[60] For St. Augustine's doctrine concerning evil, see G. Philips, *La raison d'être du mal d'après saint Augustin* (Louvain 1927). For similar ideas in another African author, cf. E. Schulze, *Das Übel in der Welt nach der Lehre des Arnobius* (Diss. Jena 1896).

[61] Cf. Gen. 2. 17.

[62] Tamquam *in umbra vitae*, writes St. Augustine. Of course, *umbra vitae* could also be taken as signifying a "foreshadow, approximation, adumbration of life (eternal)"; thus the German translator Mitterer, 417: "Schattenbild des (ewigen) Lebens." Cf. also Heb. 8. 5, where St. Paul speaks of priests on earth as offering

umbrae . . . caelestium. But *umbra* has also the figurative meaning of " shelter," " cover," " security " (so Cicero, Livy, Quintilian) and the consequent " rest," " leisure " (Cicero, Ovid). Augustine often describes Paradise as a place where there was perfect temporal happiness, where Adam and Eve were secure from fear and want, from sickness and death; and with this state he contrasts — as he does in the present passage — the *futurum bonum* of life in heaven (cf. *De civ. Dei.* 11. 12; 14. 10; *Enarr. in Ps.* 29. 2. 17).

[63] Rom. 5. 12.

[64] At the time St. Augustine wrote the *Enchiridion*, he was still very much occupied with defending Catholic doctrine against Pelagianism. It was in this same year, 421, that he wrote his brilliant work, *Against Julian the Defender of the Pelagian Heresy.* The able and determined apostle of Pelagianism, Julian of Eclanum, had published in 419 *Four Books for Turbantius*, in which he accused Augustine of introducing Manichaeism into Catholic doctrine. He likewise rejected completely the teaching concerning original sin. For the two principals involved in this controversy, see A. Bruckner, *Die vier Bücher Julians von Aeclanum an Turbantius. Ein Beitrag zur Charakteristik Julians und Augustins* (Neue Stud. z. Gesch. d. Theol. u. Kirche 8, Berlin 1910).

[65] Rom. 9. 21: *Ex eadem massa* (ἐκ τοῦ αὐτοῦ φυράματος). Augustine ordinarily renders the word φύραμα by *massa*, rarely by *conspersio*. He always gives the term a pejorative meaning by adding certain modifiers; thus, *massa damnationis, massa perditionis, massa peccati*, etc. Cf. A. M. Jacquin, " La prédestination d'après Saint Augustin," *Miscellanea Agostiniana* 2 (Rome 1931) 862; J. Mausbach, *Die Ethik des heiligen Augustinus* (2nd ed., Freiburg i. Br. 1929) 2. 148. For further examples in the writings of St. Augustine, see *De civ. Dei* 14. 26; 21. 12; *De corrept. et grat.* 7. 12; *Serm.* 10. 1 Guelferb. (472 Morin); 18. 2 Guelferb. (501 Morin); *Ep.* 186.4; 194. 4, 14, 23, 39; etc.

[66] The idea of man himself turning evil to good, *malo bene uti*, is a favorite one with Augustine. Thus, when man uses his members to perform good works, he uses well the evil of the flesh (*De pecc. mer. et remiss.* 2. 45); when he offers his life for his fellow man, he turns the evil of death to good (*ibid.*); when husband and wife practice restraint in their conjugal life, they derive good from the evil of concupiscence (*De cont.* 27); etc. Cf. Mausbach, *op. cit.* 1. 110; 2. 180 f.

⁶⁷ Perhaps in all of St. Augustine's writings no other passage conveys a sadder picture than does this one of the ruin which the sin of Adam ushered into the world. To the extent in which this picture of man's condemnation represents his exclusion from heaven, a supernatural destiny to which he had no claim whatever, all later theology will agree that it is not overdrawn. To the extent, however, in which the passage may have been meant to describe man's consignment to the positive punishment or torture of hell, later theologians will refuse to admit its justice. Regarding Augustine's teaching concerning original sin, see especially J. Mausbach, *op. cit.* 2. 139-208; also E. Gilson, *op. cit.* 194 f., 205 f., 213.

⁶⁸ The air was regarded as the medium in which the evil spirits existed and carried on their activity. Writing to the Ephesians (2. 2), St. Paul tells them: . . . aliquando ambulastis . . . *secundum principem potestatis aeris huius.* Cf. *ibid.* 6. 12. For similar ideas in the writings of Philo and Origen, see J. Quasten, " A Coptic Counterpart of a Vision in the Acts of Perpetua and Felicitas," *Byzantion* 15 (1940-41) 3-5. Augustine's African compatriot Lactantius expresses the same opinion: cf. E. Schneweis, *Angels and Demons according to Lactantius* (Stud. in Christ. Ant. 3, Washington 1944) 106-9. Most of the early Christian writers derive their views on this point from the *Book of Enoch* 21. 10 (GCS *Das Buch Henoch,* edd. Fleming-Rademacher, 51).

⁶⁹ The theologians of a later day were to express this idea more clearly and succinctly, by saying that the angels, although created with sanctifying grace, were rewarded with an eternity of heaven only after they had proved their loyalty to God.

⁷⁰ Cf. Matt. 22. 30; Luke 20. 36.

⁷¹ Cf. Gal. 4. 26; also Apoc. 21. 2.

⁷² Cf. Isa. 54. 1 and Gal. 4. 27. The mother referred to is *Mother Church.* The passages in Galatians and Isaias inspired the early personification of the Church as a mother, as is pointed out on the first page of the study by J. C. Plumpe, *Mater Ecclesia. An Inquiry into the Concept of the Church as Mother in Early Christianity* (Stud. in Christ. Ant. 5, Washington 1943).

⁷³ It is well known that St. Augustine was convinced that the number of the saved will be quite small. This view was probably based on the observation he himself made concerning the relatively small number of *real* Christians in the world. The data of revelation on this point lead to nothing more than conjecture. See also below, § 97.

[74] Rom. 4. 17.

[75] Wisd. 11. 21.

[76] Those who claim that original sin destroyed completely man's faculty of free will, almost invariably cite in defence of their teaching this passage of the *Enchiridion*, or similar statements made by St. Augustine, for instance, in *De perf. iustit. hom.* 4. 9; *Ep.* 145. 2; *Cont. duas ep. Pelag.* 1. 4. But when he said, as he does here, that by sin man had lost free will, he means to say only what he had affirmed so clearly in his *Cont. duas ep. Pelag.* 1. 5: Quis autem nostrum dicat, quod primi hominis peccato perierit *liberum arbitrium* de humano genere? *Libertas quippe periit* per peccatum, *sed illa, quae in paradiso fuit.* This Augustinian distinction between *liberum arbitrium* and *libertas* is of capital importance. The *libertas* which was lost by sin was, according to St. Augustine, the power not to sin. This he considered the highest and truest type of freedom, which will be restored to man completely only in heaven. Cf. J. B. Faure, *op. cit.* 66; also E. Portalié, " Augustin (Saint)," *Dict. de théol. cath.* 1. 2 (Paris 1909) 2385 — 92; E. Gilson, *op. cit.* 212 n. 2.

[77] Cf. 2 Peter 2. 19. Notice the rhyme in Augustine's version of the text: a quo enim *devictus est* (Vulgate: superatus est), huic et servus *addictus est* (Vulg.: huius et servus est).

[78] Here as well as in many other passages the reader will certainly be inclined to accuse St. Augustine of teaching that the will of fallen man is free only to sin, unless he understands well that Augustine has in mind the supernatural character of the state from which man fell, and the equally supernatural character of the state to which by divine grace he is to be restored. Augustine had said that by his sin Adam had lost for us the supernatural power (*libertas*) not to sin. Obviously, then, having lost that power, we are now free to sin, but not to accomplish good, that is, supernatural good which counts for heaven, unless and until the will is again prepared for such a task by divine grace. Hence, according to St. Augustine, far from destroying free will, grace makes the use of free will possible by freeing it from the shackles of sin. Read the entire third chapter in E. Gilson, *op. cit.* 185 ff.; also H. Jonas, *Augustin und das paulinische Freiheitsproblem* (Forsch. z. Relig. u. Liter. d. A. u. N. Test., N. F. 27, Göttingen 1930); H. Barth, *Die Freiheit der Entscheidung im Denken Augustins* (Basel 1935); L. Bovy, *Grâce et liberté chez S. Augustin* (Montreal 1938); S. Pedone, *Il problema della volontà in S. Agostino* (Lanciano 1940).

[79] John 8. 36.

[80] Eph. 2. 8.

[81] 1 Cor. 7. 25.

[82] Eph. 2. 8 f.

[83] *Ibid.* 2. 10.

[84] Cf. 2 Cor. 5. 17; also Gal. 6. 15.

[85] Ps. 50. 12.

[86] Phil. 2. 13; cf. also 1 Thess. 2. 13.

[87] Rom. 9. 16.

[88] Prov. 8. 35, quoted from the Septuagint.

[89] Cf. Gilson, *op. cit.* 204-216: "La grâce et la liberté."

[90] Ps. 58. 11.

[91] *Ibid.* 22. 6.

[92] Cf. Matt. 5.44 and Phil. 2. 13.

[92a] Cf. Matt. 7. 7.

[93] The primary purpose St. Augustine had in mind when he composed this passage as a sort of commentary on Romans 9. 16, was to refute the error by which for a time he had himself been deceived and which was later on to be known as Semi-Pelagianism. To understand his thought it is necessary to know what he meant by the terms which occur so often throughout these chapters: *velle et operari*, and *velle et currere*. Faure, *op. cit.* 70-75, discusses all these points at great length and with great acumen in a note appended to §§ 31 and 32.

[94] Ps. 89.9.

[95] Job 14. 1.

[96] John 3. 36.

[97] Eph. 2. 3.

[98] Rom. 5. 10 and 9.

[99] Concerning this point, see also the initial paragraph of Augustine's *De patientia.* We are likewise reminded of the earlier work by Lactantius: *De ira Dei.* Cf. M. Pohlenz, *Vom Zorne Gottes. Eine Studie über den Einfluss der griechischen Philosophie auf das alte Christentum* (Forsch. z. Rel. u. Lit. d. A. u. N. Test. 12, Göttingen 1909).

[100] Rom. 8. 14.

[101] John 1. 14.

[102] This sense of *pars pro toto* in John 1. 14 had been denied a few decades earlier by Apollinaris, bishop of Laodicea (d. *ca.* 390).

[103] Rom. 3. 20.

[104] Augustine's insistence here on the completeness of Christ's human nature may be due at least in part to the Christological error (Apollinaris) which denied that Christ had a rational soul (cf. the next paragraph).

[105] Although the doctrine of the perpetual virginity of Mary may justly be called a dogma of secondary importance as compared with that of belief in God the Rewarder, in the Trinity and the Incarnation, it is worthy of note that it is stressed over and over again by St. Augustine, as it was by the great writers of the second and third centuries. He calls Mary *concipiens virgo, pariens virgo, virgo gravida, virgo feta, virgo perpetua.* Cf. *De Trin.* 8. 7; *Serm.* 186. 1; 188. 4. See J. G. Machen, *The Virgin Birth of Christ* (London 1930).

[106] For the development of this comparison between *Mater Ecclesia* and *Mater Dei*, see F. J. Dölger, "Die Inschrift im Baptisterium S. Giovanni in Fonte an der Lateranensischen Basilika aus der Zeit Xystus III (432-440) und die Symbolik des Taufbrunnens bei Leo dem Grossen," *Ant. u. Christ.* 2 (1930) 252-57.

[107] In the collection of St. Augustine's letters the composition referred to is No. 137, also known by the title *De Incarnatione.* It was written in the year 412 upon special request. Volusianus had informed Augustine that the problems of the Incarnation and the abiding virginity of Mary had been brought up at a gathering of friends, and that he and some of his companions had put off the questioner until the matter could be referred to Augustine for clarification (cf. Volusianus' letter to Augustine, *Ep.* 135).

[108] John 1. 1.

[109] Cf. *ibid.* 10. 30.

[110] Cf. *ibid.* 14. 28.

[111] St. Augustine's teaching on Christology is a masterpiece of dogmatic exposition. His explanations are given with such soundness and vigor and clarity that the great heresies of Nestorius and Eutyches, which were soon to arise after his death, never gained a real foothold in the Western Church.

[112] Phil. 2. 6. *Rapina* (ἁρπαγμός) has received various interpretations from Catholic scholars. Some maintain that St. Paul meant by it a possession which one might seek greedily to retain, and hence the text would read: Christ did not seek avidly to retain the glory to which, being equal to God (the Father), He had a right, but emptied Himself. Others translate the word to signify an excuse

to escape something unpleasant, and accordingly we have this reading: Christ did not wish to use His equality with God as a pretext to escape from obeying the command of His Father to become man. A third rendition for *rapina* is something undue. It is in this sense that St. Augustine accepts it, conveying therefore the idea that Christ did not look upon equality with God (the Father) as something to which He had no right: He " thought it not robbery to be equal with *God*." Cf. H. Schumacher, *Christus in seiner Präexistenz und Kenose* 1 (Rome 1914) 17-129; Prat, *op. cit.* 380 f., 538-40.

[113] Phil. 2. 7.

[114] Lege Scripturas, nunquam invenies de Christo dictum quod *adoptivus* sit *Filius Dei* (*Cont. Secund. Man.* 5).

[115] In this section there are striking parallels to phrasings in the so-called Athanasian Creed; e. g., *Christus Iesus Dei Filius est Deus et homo. Deus ante* omnia *saecula,* homo *in* nostro *saeculo* (Aug.) ~ *Iesus Christus, Dei Filius, Deus et homo est. Deus* est ex substantia Patris *ante saecula* genitus, et *homo* est ex substantia matris *in saeculo natus* (Ath. Cr.); accessit Verbo *anima rationalis et caro* (Aug.) ~ *ex anima rationali et humana carne* subsistens (Ath. Cr.). The Athanasian Creed, also known as the *Quicumque*, certainly was not composed by St. Athanasius. It is of much more recent Latin origin. For numerous other parallels in the writings of St. Augustine, cf. F. J. Badcock, *The History of the Creeds* (London 1930) 199.

[116] Here again Augustine shows his superb grasp of the deeper meaning of the hypostatic union, or the union of two natures, the divine and the human, in the one Person of the Word. Not many years after this was written, Nestorius, the patriarch of Constantinople, in the heresy that bears his name denied the union of two natures in the one Person of the God-Man Christ.

[117] Note the distinction, insisted on frequently by St. Augustine, between merits *antecedent to justification* or liberation from the *massa peccati* created by the fall of Adam, and merits *antecedent to salvation* or the gaining of heaven. Here and in the following Augustine proves the completely gratuitous character of the grace by which men are freed from the *massa damnationis* by comparing the process with that of the gratuitous bestowal of graces made by the Blessed Trinity to the human nature of Christ.

[118] Luke 1. 28 and 30.

[119] John 1. 14.

[120] *Donum Dei* ("Gift of God") is a common Scriptural term for the Holy Spirit; cf. John 4. 10 (Christ to the Samaritan woman): Si scires *donum Dei*, et quis est . . . tu forsitan petisses ab eo, et dedisset tibi aquam vivam; also Acts 2. 38; 8. 20. For other passages in Augustine, see J. P. Christopher's note in Augustine, *De cat. rud.* 20. 35: ACW 2 (1946) 132 n. 222. See also M. Schmaus, *Die psychologische Trinitätslehre des. hl. Augustinus* (Münst. Beitr. z. Theol. 11, Münster i. W. 1927) 392-99.

[121] Luke 1. 35.

[122] Matt. 1. 20.

[123] Augustine, following here, as usual, the Apostolic Creed as formulated at Milan, has *et* ("and") virgine Maria, not *ex* ("of") virgine Maria, which he has in one instance, *Serm.* 215 — presupposing the Apostolic Creed as formulated in the African Church. Cf. A. Hahn, *Bibliothek der Symbole und Glaubensregeln der alten Kirche* (ed. by G. L. Hahn, Breslau 1897) 39 nn. 41 and 42, 58 n. 107.

[124] John 1. 3.

[125] Rom. 1. 3.

[126] St. Augustine arrives at this conclusion from the numerical oneness of the divine nature possessed by the three divine Persons: ubi nulla naturarum nulla est diversitas voluntatum (*Cont. Maxim.* 2. 10. 2). All later theology expresses the same thought in the axiom: *omnia ad extra sunt Tribus communia.*

[127] Cf. above, n. 72.

[128] The learned bishop spent much time and effort to explain why it is that Christ is not the son of the Holy Spirit. St. Thomas took up the question in his *Summa* 3. q. 32, a. 3, and adopted substantially the solution offered here: Solum illud, quod generatur in *similitudinem generantis, filiationis* accipit *nomen.*

[129] Cf. Matt. 23. 15; also 1 John 3. 10.

[130] Cf. Matt. 8. 12 and 13. 38.

[131] For the same idea, see Augustine, *In Ioan. Ev. tract.* 111. 5.

[132] Cf. above, n. 120.

[133] Rom. 8. 3.

[134] Although St. Augustine's reputation as a scholar does not rest on his power of Biblical interpretation, he gives here a very clear and exact explanation of a text which many have found difficult, and because of which many found it necessary to teach that Christ really became the universal sinner, and that He redeemed us by

becoming the object of the Father's vengeance. Augustine always insisted that Christ redeemed us by becoming our High Priest and by offering to the Blessed Trinity the perfect sacrifice for sin.

[135] Cf. Osee 4. 8.

[136] Cf. 2 Cor. 5. 20 f.

[137] The *font* — the *sepulchre*: It is well known that for many centuries the ordinary, but not exclusive, method of baptizing was by immersion. Like St. Paul, Augustine here clearly supposes immersion, that is, descent into the pool and ascent therefrom, in likeness to Christ's descent into the sepulchre and His ascent therefrom in His glorious Resurrection. Cf. *Ambrose, De sacr.* 2. 7. 15 (150 Quasten): cum enim mergis, mortis suscipis et sepulturae similitudinem, Cyril of Jer., *Cat. myst.* 2. 4; Basil, *De spir. sanct.* 15. 35.

[138] In this work St. Augustine makes it perfectly clear that no one can be saved unless he receives the remission of original sin, and that the sacrament of baptism is the ordinary means by which that sin is washed away. However, in other works he recognizes substitutes for the sacrament, for instance, martyrdom, or even faith and conversion of heart, when the reception of the sacrament is impossible. Cf. *De peccat. mer. et remiss.* 1. 23; *De bapt.* 4. 29; *Cont. litt. Petil.* 2. 52.

[139] In St. Augustine's home country, North Africa, infant baptism had become the usual practice as early as the middle of the third century; cf. St. Cyprian, *Ep.* 64. 2. See F. van der Meer, *Augustinus de Zielzorger* (Utrecht 1947) 308-311: "Nooddoop en Kinderdoop."

[140] Vergil, *Aen.* 2. 20.

[141] Num. 21. 7. Augustine follows the Septuagint which has the singular τὸν ὄφιν. The Vulgate has *serpentes*, "serpents." The incident of the murmuring Jews being punished by the fiery serpents is referred to elsewhere in Augustine's writings, although apparently he does not quote Num. 21. 7 again. The present instance is therefore an interesting case in point to illustrate his remarkable mastery of Sacred Scripture. Cf. below, n. 408.

[142] Matt. 2. 20.

[143] Exod. 32. 31.

[144] *Ibid.* 32. 4.

[145] Rom. 5. 12.

[146] Deut. 5. 9.

[147] Ezech. 18. 2; also Jer. 31. 29.

[148] This reference to penance does not necessarily indicate the sacrament of penance.

[149] Ps. 50. 7.

[150] Augustine takes back nothing of what he had affirmed just before. His doubt does not bear on the question of fact, but only on the question of the extent to which the sins of parents are visited upon their children.

[151] 1 Tim. 2. 5.

[152] Luke 3. 4; cf. Isa. 40. 3.

[153] Mark 1. 8.

[154] However, the words reported by Matthew (3. 17; cf. also Luke 3. 22) were: *This is my beloved son, in whom I am well pleased.* St. Augustine had in mind Ps. 2. 7; cf. also Acts 13.33 and Heb. 1. 5; 5. 5.

[155] That one of the purposes of the Incarnation was the manifestation of humility through God made man is an idea that receives great emphasis in many of Augustine's works. In fact, the mystery of the Incarnation is sometimes referred to as *humilitas*; cf. J. P. Christopher's observations on Augustine, *De cat. rud.* 19. 33: ACW 2 (1946) 130 n. 206. See also L. De Grandmaison, *Jésus Christ* (2nd ed., Paris 1928) 2. 636. For texts from the writings of Augustine on this point, consult O. Scheel, *Die Anschauung Augustins über Christi Person und Werk* (Tübingen 1901) 347 ff.

[156] Note the wordplay consisting of the repetition of the same verb with varying inflection (= polyptoton): non *miseranda* necessitate, sed *miserante* potius voluntate.

[157] Rom. 5. 16.

[158] *Ibid.* 5. 18.

[159] Here, that is, in baptism.

[160] Rom. 6. 1.

[161] *Ibid.* 5. 18.

[162] *Ibid.* 6. 2.

[163] *In Christo Iesu* — For the use and meaning of this expression in the letters of St. Paul, see Prat, *op. cit.*, 2. 476-80.

[164] Rom. 6. 3.

[165] *Ibid.* 6. 4-11.

[166] Gal. 5. 24. Augustine, following the Greek σὺν τοῖς παθήμασιν, here reads *cum passionibus* for *cum vitiis* of the Vulgate. Concerning the borrowed word *passio*, Augustine wrote in *De nupt. et conc.* 2. 55: *passio* in lingua Latina, maxime in usu loquendi ecclesiastico, non nisi ad vituperationem consuevit intellegi. It is interesting to observe that in the case of the present passage Augus-

tine apparently always wrote *cum passionibus* (cf. *De cont.* 9; *In Ioan. Ev. tract.* 120. 9), while before him Cyprian wrote *cum vitiis* (*De hab. virg.* 6). Concerning Augustine's critical treatment of the Bible, notably the Pauline epistles, cf. the excellent study by D. De Bruyne, "Saint Augustin reviseur de la Bible," *Miscellanea Agostiniana* 2 (Rome 1931) 521-606.

[167] Rom. 6. 4.

[168] *Ibid.*

[169] Col. 3. 1-3.

[170] *Ibid.* 3. 4.

[171] 2 Tim. 4. 1; cf. Acts 10.42, Rom. 9. 12, 1 Peter 4. 5.

[172] John 5. 29.

[173] Ps. 53. 3.

[174] *Ibid.* 42. 1.

[175] Gal. 4. 26. The reference in the celebrated allegory is of course to the Church (cf. above, n. 72).

[176] Cf. 1 Tim. 3. 15.

[177] Cf. Ps. 112. 3.

[178] Cf. Apoc. 14. 3.

[178a] The thought that the angels help us as they should, is beautifully amplified in the *De doctrina Christiana* (1. 31-33). Here St. Augustine establishes that the command of love of our neighbor binds men and angels to a mutual affection.

[179] Cf. Ps. 81.6 (also John 10. 34 f.): Ego dixi *dii estis* et filii excelsi omnes.

[180] *Regula fidei* (κανὼν τῆς πίστεως), the ancient term for the profession of faith made by the candidate for baptism. For other passages in which St. Augustine uses *regula fidei* = creed (*symbolum*), see C. Mohrmann, *Die altchristliche Sondersprache in den Sermones des hl. Augustin* (Lat. Christ. prim. 3, Nijmegen 1932) 142. — For the history of the African Creed, see F. J. Badcock, "Le credo primitif d'Afrique," *Rev. Bén.* 45 (1933) 3-9. Cf. also F. J. Dölger, "Die Eingliederung des Taufsymbols in den Taufvollzug nach den Schriften Tertullians," *Ant. u. Christ.* 4 (1934) 138-46.

[181] 1 Cor. 6. 19.

[182] *Ibid.* 6. 15.

[183] 1 Cor. 3. 16.

[184] Col. 1. 18 and John 2. 19.

[185] 2 Peter 2. 4.

[186] Heb. 1. 13.

[187] Ps. 148. 2.

[188] Col. 1. 16.

[189] For some interesting examples of the equating of stars and angels in ancient magical invocations, cf. J. Barbel, *Christos Angelos* (Theophaneia 3, Bonn 1941) 219-21.

[190] Zach. 1. 9.

[191] Matt. 1. 20.

[192] The reference is to Abraham offering to wash the feet of his angelic guests appearing to him in the valley of Mambre (Gen. 18. 4); and to Lot who invited the two angels coming to him at Sodom: *lavate pedes vestros* (*ibid.* 19. 2).

[193] Cf. Gen. 32. 24 ff.

[194] St. Augustine has already owned (§ 58) that he is unable to arrive at a clear classification of the angels. Here again he refuses to indulge in idle speculation concerning the possibility of angels having a certain corporeity or bodily attributes. He practically brushes the question aside as being unimportant. Characteristically, among Augustine's numerous treatises there is none on the angels.

[195] Cf. 2 Cor. 11. 14.

[196] Rom. 8. 31 f.

[197] Cf. Augustine, *Serm.* 12. 2 Guelferb. (480 Morin): Pro ipsis qui ceciderunt angelis homines illuc venturi sunt, et *implebunt locum eorum qui ceciderunt.* In *De civ. Dei* 22. 1, Augustine speaks of the possibility that these replacements will even exceed the number of the fallen angels. Cf. E. Peterson, *Il libro degli angeli* (Rome 1946) 40 n. 70.

[198] Eph. 1. 10.

[199] Here and in the following we are reminded (cf. P. Simon, 162 f.) of the very great rôle that the concept of *pax* — peace — plays in the plan of St. Augustine's *De civitate Dei*; note, for example, 19.10 ff.; 19. 26 f.; 22. 29. For a study of these thoughts in the light of previous sentiment (*Pax Augusta*, etc.), cf. H. Fuchs, *Augustin und der antike Friedensgedanke* (Neue philol. Unters. 3, Berlin 1926). When Augustine wrote the *Enchiridion* (421), the City of God was still an unfinished manuscript (wr. 413-26). Here we have one of the many instances in which Augustine's all-absorbing occupation with his masterpiece is reflected in treatises wrested from his pen by special request.

[200] Col. 1. 19 f.

[201] Phil. 4. 7.

[202] 1 Cor. 13. 12.

[203] Cf. Luke 20. 36.

[204] 1 Cor. 13. 12.

[205] Luke 15. 24.

[206] Rom. 8. 14.

[207] Cf. Wisd. 9. 15.

[208] Theology owes much to Augustine's distinction and clarification of lesser, venial sins (*peccata quotidiana, minuta, venialia*), as contrasted with greater, mortal sins (here called *crimina*). Read the interesting instruction which he gave (*Ep.* 104. 13 ff.) to the bishop Nestorius for whom all sins were alike (*Ep.* 103. 3). The subject of St. Augustine's teaching on venial sin is treated by J. Mausbach, *Die Ethik des heiligen Augustinus* (2nd ed., Freiburg i. Br. 1929) 1. 235-41.

[209] 1 John 1. 8.

[210] That is, those excommunicated from the Church because of the commission of a capital sin — apostasy, homicide, or adultery. The "measure of time" mentioned in the following refers to the length of time during which such sinners performed *public* penance.

[211] Ps. 50. 19.

[212] *Ibid.* 37. 10.

[213] Cf. 2 Cor. 1. 22 and Eph. 1. 14.

[214] For the interpretation of this passage, see K. Adam, *Die geheime Kirchenbusse nach dem hl. Augustin* (Kempten 1921) 66; P. Galtier, *L'Eglise et la rémission des péchés aux premiers siècles* (Paris 1932) 3602ff.; B. Poschmann, *Kirchenbusse und correptio secreta bei Augustinus* (Braunsberg 1923) 26.

[215] Eccli. 40. 1.

[216] In this passage St. Augustine is speaking of satisfaction for sin which can be made during our life on earth. Later on in this work he will discuss the problem of satisfaction to be made in the life to come.

[217] 1 Cor. 11. 31 f.

[217a] This entire chapter is quoted by Augustine in his *De octo Dulcitii quaest.* 1. 10-13.

[218] Who are these Catholics? St. Augustine refrains from mentioning any names. Cf. *De civ. Dei* 21. 17 ff. Some think that St. Jerome and St. Ambrose held this erroneous opinion. Cf. J. Tixeront, *History of Dogmas* (trans. by H. L. B., St. Louis 1914) 2. 339, 343 ff.

[219] *De fide et operibus*, written early in the year 413.

[220] Gal. 5. 6.

[221] James 2. 17.

[222] *Ibid.* 2. 14.

[223] 1 Cor. 3. 15.

[224] *Ibid.* 6. 9 f.

[225] Cf. *ibid.* 3. 11-15.

[226] *Ibid.*

[227] Eccli. 27. 6.

[228] 1 Cor. 7. 32.

[229] *Ibid.* 7. 33.

[230] St. Augustine gives the same interpretation of 1 Cor. 3. 11 ff. in *De fide et op.* 16. 27; *De civ. Dei.* 21. 26; *Enarr. in Ps.* 29, *serm.* 2. 9; *ibid.* 80. 21.

[231] It might well seem from the opening words of this passage that St. Augustine looked upon the existence of purgatory not as a part of Christian faith but as an opinion more or less probable. However, there should be no serious question about his belief in a state of purgation after this life, for nothing else can explain his constant insistence on the need of praying for the dead. But it is one thing to believe that there is a purgatory, and another to believe that the fire of purgatory is real fire. It is this latter point which Augustine considers to be a matter of probability and the object of free discussion.

[232] 1 Cor. 6. 10.

[233] Cf. *De civ. Dei.* 21. 26. 4.

[234] Matt. 25. 34 and 41. The giving of alms played a most important role in both the life and the teaching of the early Church. St. Augustine's fellow African, St. Cyprian, wrote a special treatise on the subject: *De opere et eleemosynis* (*ca.* 253). In this work (2) Cyprian wrote concerning the efficacy of almsgiving, comparing it with that of baptism: *sicut lavacro aquae salutaris gehennae ignis extinguitur, ita eleemosynis atque operationibus iustis delictorum flamma sopitur.* Cf. Galtier, *op. cit.* 47 f. In subapostolic times the Christians were admonished to give alms from the fruit of their labor and thus free themselves from the guilt of sin: see *Didache* 4. 6 f.; *Ep. Barnabae* 19. 10; Hermas, *Pastor, mand.* 2. 4-7. Cf. also A. T. Geoghegan, *The Attitude toward Labor in Early Christianity and Ancient Culture* (Stud. in Christ. Ant. 6, Washington 1945) 116, 125, 132.

[235] Eccli. 15. 21.

[236] This passage reminds us of 1 John 1. 8: "If we say that we have no sin, we do deceive ourselves, and the truth is not in us," and of James 3. 2: "For in many things we all offend."

[237] Matt. 6. 9.

[238] *Ibid.* 6. 12.

[239] Luke 11. 41.

[240] *Ibid.* 6. 27.

[241] Matt. 6. 12.

[242] Here St. Augustine makes a clear-cut distinction between the precepts and the counsels.

[243] John 14. 6.

[244] Matt. 6. 14 f.

[245] Luke 11. 41.

[246] *Ibid.* 11. 37-41.

[247] Acts 15. 9.

[248] Titus 1. 15. This verse, and especially its sententious beginning served Augustine in the formulation of many arguments. Cf. J. C. Plumpe, "Omnia Munda Mundis," *Theol. Stud.* 6 (1945) 509-23.

[249] Eccli. 30. 24.

[250] Rom. 5. 16.

[251] *Ibid.* 5. 8.

[252] Cf. Luke 11. 42.

[253] *Ibid.* 10. 27.

[254] For this and the following, cf. *ibid.* 11. 42.

[255] Cf. Matt. 23. 26.

[256] Ps. 10. 5.

[257] Ps. 58. 11.

[258] 1 Cor. 7. 6.

[259] *Ibid.* St. Augustine voices this severe opinion regarding intercourse in marriage on several other occasions. See *De bono coniug.* 6: Coniugalis enim concubitus generandi gratia non habet culpam, *concupiscentiae vero satiandae, sed tamen cum coniuge, propter tori fidem venialem habet culpam.* Cf. *ibid.* 13. 15; *De bono vid.* 5; *De nupt. et conc.* 1. 16.; *Cont. Iul. Pel.* 3. 43; *De doctr. Christ.* 3. 27; *Serm.* 278. 9. Most of the early Christian writers shared this view, a notable exception being St. John Chrysostom, *De virg.* 19, 29, and *passim.* Consult D. Lindner, *Der Usus Matrimonii. Seine sittliche Bewertung in katholischer Moraltheologie alter und neuer Zeit* (Munich 1929) 57 ff. The interpretation by all these authors

is incorrect. *Secundum veniam*, the version we have here, or *secundum indulgentiam*, as the Vulgate translates it, means a concession of something *less perfect*, but *not sinful*, since sin cannot be conceded or permitted.

[260] *Ibid.* 6. 1.

[261] *Ibid.* 6. 4-6.

[262] *Ibid.* 6. 7.

[263] *Ibid.*

[264] Matt. 5. 40.

[265] Luke 6. 30.

[266] James 3. 2.

[267] Matt. 5. 22.

[268] *Ibid.* 5. 23. Cf. *Serm.* 82. 35.

[269] Concerning the belief in astrologers as recorded by the Roman historians and satirists, and the superstitious practices among the Africans in Augustine's time, see the interesting note by J. P. Christopher, ACW 2 (1946) 107 n. 79.

[270] Cf. Gal. 4. 10. Augustine, it is said (cf. the German translation of the *Enchiridion* by S. Mitterer, 467 n. 4), appears to have misunderstood this passage in which St. Paul primarily castigated the continued observance of the Jewish law, as advocated by certain Judaisers among the Galatians. However, the Apostle uses very general terms and he may very well have meant to refer also to pagan practices as well as to superstitious observances inspired by astrology, such as St. Augustine has in mind here. Cf. M. J. Lagrange, *Saint Paul, Epître aux Galates* (3rd ed., Paris 1926) 108 f. Cf. Augustine, *Ep.* 55. 12 and 13.

[271] *Ibid.* 4. 11.

[272] Ps. 9 B. 3. The new Latin translation of the Psalms (Rome 1945) reads *peccator gloriatur* (" the sinner boasts of ") for *laudatur peccator* (" the sinner is praised ").

[273] Isa. 5. 7. The vineyard is identified in the present verse as " the house of Israel."

[274] Gen. 18. 20.

[275] Cf. *Cont. ep. Parm.* 3. 13 ff.; *Ep.* 95. 3. 17; *Serm.* 17. 3.

[276] Gal. 4. 11.

[277] *Ep. ad Gal. exp.* 35.

[278] Cf. *Quaest. in Heptateuch.* 4. 24 ff.; *De lib. arb.* 3. 18. 55 ff., *De div. quaest.* 83. 26; *De pecc. mer. et remiss.* 1. 39. 70; *ibid.* 2. 17. 26; *De nat. et grat.* 67. 81; *Cont. duas ep. Pelag.* 1. 3. 7; *ibid.* 1. 13. 27.

[278a] Matt. 6. 12 f. Cf. below, n. 377.

[279] Ps. 26. 1.

[280] Augustine has often been accused of teaching that fallen man commits sin by necessity. Were it so, it would be quite impossible to understand his exhortation to pray so that we may be kept from sin. The truth is that he always taught that we can avoid sin, but only with the help of God's grace. Typical of this belief is the classical passage in *De nat. et grat.* 43. 50: Non igitur Deus impossibilia iubet, sed iubendo admonet, *et facere quod possis, et petere quod non possis.*

[281] It is difficult to say for what species of sins severe penance was demanded. Generally, Augustine considers that all those grave sins which according to the Scriptures exclude from the kingdom of God (1 Cor. 6. 9 f.; Gal. 5. 19 f.) belong to this class. Cf. *Serm.* 351. 7; *De fide et op.* 26. 48. St. Augustine enumerates such sins in *Serm.* 56. 8. 12; *De cat. rud.* (cf. ACW 2. 79 f.). In *Spec. de script. sacr.* 29 he explicitly rejects the idea that there are only three grave sins. Cf. J. Mausbach, *op. cit.* 1. 230-35.

[282] "*To humble himself*": this indicates quite clearly that the performance of this type of penance must have been a more or less public act (cf. *Serm.* 278. 12). Tertullian mentions (*De paen.* 10.) that the attendant humiliation kept many from doing penance.

[283] 2 Tim. 2. 25.

[284] Luke 22. 61.

[285] Cf. Matt. 12. 32; Luke 12. 10. For the "Sin against the Holy Spirit," see E. Mangenot, "Blasphème contre le Saint-Esprit," *Dict. de théol. cath.* 2. 1 (1910) 911-16; M. J. Lagrange, *Evangile selon saint Matthieu* (Paris 1923) 244 f.; B. Poschmann, *Paenitentia secunda* (Theophaneia 1, Bonn 1940) 13 f.; 427 f.

[286] By the "little book" he means his *Sermo 71.*

[287] Saint Augustine tells us in *Enarr. in Ps.* 88. 5 that the doctrine of the resurrection of the body had met with violent opposition on the part of pagans, even of those who believed in the immortality of the soul: *In nulla re tam vehementer, tam pertinaciter, tam obnixe et contentiose contradicitur fidei Christianae sicut de carnis resurrectione.* We need but recall that to Platonic thinking the union of soul and matter is contrary to nature; that the soul exists in the body as in a prison house from which it wishes to be delivered. Again, Manichaeism—which also had played a most prominent rôle in Augustine's long search for truth—postulated that all matter is evil

and that therefore man's good soul, as distinguished from his evil soul, is in constant conflict with the evil body it inhabits. See *De civ. Dei* 22. 12-20 and *Serm.* 361, where Augustine gathers together all the objections of the pagan opposition and refutes them with great care.

[288] The reference is of course to baptism.

[289] The problem which Augustine discusses in this passage is intimately bound up with the question whether the embryo is a human being. According to Roman law a child could not be called a human being before it had been born. However, we know from ancient Christian writers that Christianity regarded the embryo as *homo*. Cf. J. Quasten, "A Roman Law of Egyptian Origin in the *Passio Perpetuae et Felicitatis*," *The Jurist* 1 (1944) 1-6; M. Roberti, "Nasciturus pro iam nato habetur nelle fonti christiane primitive," in M. Roberti — E. Bussi — G. Vismara, *Christianesimo e diritto romano* (Milan 1935) 65 ff.; F. J. Dölger, "Das Lebensrecht des ungeborenen Kindes und die Fruchtabtreibung in der Bewertung der heidnischen und christlichen Antike," *Ant. u. Christ.* 4 (1933) 1-61.

[290] I read (with Cornish and Raulx) *ne matres* (obj.) ... *occidant*, not *ne matres* (subj.) *occidant* (Shaw, Mitterer, Simon). The idea that a fetus unfortunately lodged is a potential *slayer* of the mother is also found with Tertullian who calls it a *matricida* (*De anima* 25). For a discussion of these passages, cf. Dölger, *loc. cit.* 44-49.

[291] St. Jerome, *Ep.* 72. 2, reports the case of a human monster with two heads, four hands, one stomach, and two feet, as having been born at Lydda in Palestine. — Jerome had died only a year or two before Augustine wrote the present treatise.

[292] In a sermon delivered on Ascension Day, Augustine stated (*Serm.* 264. 6): Ista caro resurget, ista ipsa quae sepelitur, quae moritur; ista quae videtur, quae palpatur, cui opus est manducare et bibere ut /possit durare; quae aegrotat, quae dolores patitur, ipsa habet resurgere, malis ad poenas sempiternas, bonis autem ut commutentur. — Long before him the Apologists were accustomed to argue that it is easier for God to restore man's body on the last day than it was to create it in the first place out of nothing. See Minucius Felix, *Oct.* 34. 9; Tertullian, *Apol.* 48. 6; Lactantius, *Inst.* 7. 23. 5.

[293] The Bishop of Hippo presents here and in the following pages an interesting and perhaps illuminating view concerning the identity of the body; for if it is the rational soul as such that gives indi-

viduality to the body to which it is joined, the problem of the identity of the risen body is greatly simplified. For a presentation of this view in modern times, see L. Billot, *De novissimis* (3rd ed., Rome 1908) 168-84.

[294] *Animale* ("animate") — *anima* ("soul"), corresponding to *spiritale* ("spiritual") — *spiritus* ("spirit").

[295] Gal. 5. 17.

[296] 1 Cor. 15. 50.

[297] *Ibid.* 15. 44.

[298] Cf. above, n. 65.

[299] 1 Tim. 2. 5.

[300] Cf. Apoc. 2. 11; 20. 6 and 14; 21. 8.

[301] It is true that at one time St. Augustine hesitated, not indeed to exclude unbaptized infants from heaven, but to affirm that on dying they undergo the positive punishment of hell. See, for instance, *De lib. arb.* 3. 23 (wr. 388-395). However, he seems never to have been able to convince himself of this, and later on he unquestionably taught, as he most certainly does here, the positive damnation of these unbaptized infants. See J. B. Faure, *op. cit.* 176. Since the time of St. Thomas, theologians have been unanimous in rejecting this severe view.

[302] Ps. 100. 1.

[303] This thought may well be called the foundation on which all Augustinian ideas concerning the saved and the lost will rest. Obviously, for Augustine the real difficulty lay not in the problem of free will and grace, nor in that of good works and grace, but in the free determination of God to show *unmerited mercy* to some and to others *merited judgment.*

[304] Here the word *virtutes* is used for "miracles." Augustine also employs the word *magnalia* in the same sense. Cf. C. Mohrmann, *Die altchristliche Sondersprache in den Sermones des heiligen Augustin* (Lat. Christ. prim. 3. 1, Nijmegen 1932) 121 f. Both terms derive from Scripture: *magnalia* (μεγαλεῖα) *Domini, Dei* — Exod. 14. 13, 2 Mac. 3. 34, Acts 2. 11, etc.; *virtutes* (δυνάμεις) — Matt. 7. 22, Luke 7. 13, 1 Cor. 12. 10, Gal. 3. 5, etc. Cf. O. Schmitz, "Der Begriff δύναμις bei Paulus," *Festgabe A. Deissmann* (Tübingen 1927) 139-67.

[305] Matt. 11. 21.

[306] "Had *He* so willed it" = *si vellet*, with some manuscripts reading *si vellent* = "had *they* so willed it." The dogmatic implica-

tions of these divergent readings are evident. Near the close of the seventeenth century, when the Benedictines of St. Maur were preparing their monumental edition of St. Augustine's works, the passage became the subject of acrimonious controversy. The manuscript authority and the context certainly favor the reading *si vellet*. Cf. O. Rottmanner, *Geistesfrüchte aus der Klosterzelle* (Munich 1908) 99-103; O. Scheel, *Augustins Enchiridion*, 76 f.; P. Simon, *op. cit.* 170 f.

[307] Ps. 113B. 3 and 134. 6.

[308] Cf. R. Jolivet, *Le problème du mal d'après S. Augustin* (Paris 1936); C. Terzi, *Il problema del male nella polemica antimanichea di S. Agostino* (Udine 1937).

[309] Even if St. Augustine does not use the terms of *antecedent* and *consequent wills* of God, unless we accept the ideas which these terms represent it is impossible to understand his thought here and in many other passages, particularly, when he is dealing with the problem of predestination.

[310] 1 Tim. 2. 4.

[311] Matt. 23. 37.

[312] Cf. L. Bovy, *Grâce et liberté chez S. Augustin* (Montreal 1938).

[313] Ps. 134. 6.

[314] Rom. 9. 18.

[315] *Ibid.* 9. 11 f.; cf. Gen. 25. 23.

[316] *Ibid.* 9. 13, quoted from Mal. 1. 2f.

[317] *Ibid.* 9. 14.

[318] Cf. A. A. Saint-Martin, *La pensée de Saint Augustin sur la prédestination* (Paris 1930); M. De Lama, *S. Augustini doctrina de gratia et praedestinatione* (Turin 1934); A. Polman, *De predestinatie van Augustinus, Thomas van Aquino en Calvijn* (Franeker 1936).

[319] See K. Kolb, *Menschliche Freiheit und göttliches Vorherwissen nach Augustin* (Freiburg i. Br. 1908).

[320] Rom. 9. 15, from Exod. 33. 19.

[321] *Ibid.* 9. 16.

[322] Eph. 2. 3.

[323] 2 Cor. 10. 17; 1 Cor. 1. 31; Jer. 9. 23 f.

[324] Rom. 9. 17; cf. Exod. 9. 16.

[325] *Ibid.* 9. 18.

[326] *Concreverat*, from *concernere* (=" to sift, mix together "), not from *concrescere* (= " to make grow together," thus Cornish, Mit-

terer, and Simon). See also *Conf.* 5. 10. 20: Talem igitur naturam eius (Salvatoris) nasci non posse de Maria Virgine arbitrabar, nisi carni *concerneretur.* Cf. J. Gibb — W. Montgomery, *The Confessions of St. Augustine* (Cambridge 1908) 129, note; also *Thes. ling. Lat.* 4 *s. v.*

[327] Rom. 9. 19.

[328] *Ibid.* 9. 20 f.

[329] Whenever St. Augustine speaks of predestination without any qualification, as he does here and elsewhere in this book, he has in mind the human race not prior to the disaster of sin, but as it had become through the commission of original sin. This is what writers like O. Rottmanner, *op. cit.* 7, mean when they say that Augustine's theory of predestination might well be called *infralapsarian.* As such, it differs widely from the predestination taught by Calvin, as A. Harnack points out, *op. cit.* 5. 216.

[330] Cf. Rom. 3. 19 and 1 Cor. 1. 31.

[331] Ps. 110. 2.

[332] St. Augustine evidently speaks of a predestination to punishment and to eternal punishment, as he does, for instance in *De anima et eius orig.* 4. 11. 16: Quos *praedestinavit ad aeternam mortem.* However, he never says that anyone is *predestined to sin.* Cf. *ibid.* 1. 7. 7: Praescientia . . . Dei . . . peccatores praenoscit, non facit." For other texts, see O. Rottmanner, *op. cit.* 18. 1.

[333] Cf. Matt. 16. 23.

[334] Cf. Acts 21. 8 ff. The incident referred to took place in the year 57 at Caesarea, in the home of Philip the evangelist. For a delightful description, see J. Holzner, *Paulus, ein Heldenleben im Dienste Christi* (2d ed., Freiburg i. Br. 1937) 340 f.

[335] *Exercens martyrem Christi.* For Augustine the term *martyr* has become less comprehensive than for Tertullian and Cyprian. These earlier writers sometimes also applied the title to *confessores* who had shown themselves "witnesses" (the term here used by Cornish and Shaw for *martyr*, with M. Raulx writing "confesseur") for Christ by submitting to torture, without dying as a result of their sufferings. But in Augustine's time death for the faith was always implied in the word *martyr* (Cf. C. Mohrmann, *op. cit.* 122-24). St. Paul's bitter experiences in Jerusalem in the year 57 were to prepare him for his actual martyrdom ten years later.

[336] 1 Tim. 2. 4. This statement by St. Paul proved to be the great difficulty in St. Augustine's teaching on predestination. The present

chapter gives ample evidence of his discomfiture, not to mention
that he gave at least three different interpretations of the passage.
For Augustine this must stand: God's will cannot be frustrated, its
efficacy can never be contingent upon human will. B. Bartmann,
Lehrbuch der Dogmatik 2 (7th ed., Freiburg i. Br. 1929) 50, rightly
speaks of Augustine's "torturous" efforts to reconcile St. Paul's
words with his own teaching in this matter, and rightly suggests
that it is quite unnecessary to refer the great bishop's earlier, *uni-
versalistic* interpretation of the passage to what theologians of another
day termed God's *antecedent* will, and his later, restrictive interpretation to His *consequent* or *absolute* will. See also A. M. Jacquin,
"La prédestination d'après Saint Augustin," *Misc. Agost.* 2 (1931)
868 f.; L. Capéran, *Le problème du salut des infidèles* (Paris 1912)
128; P. Simon, *op. cit.* 173.

[337] John 1.9.
[338] 1 Tim. 2.2.
[339] *Ibid.* 2.3.
[340] *Ibid.* 2.4.
[341] Luke 11.42.
[342] Ps. 134.6.
[343] In *De civ. Dei* 20.30.1, 3, 4, St. Augustine gives the reason
for this inability to choose evil notwithstanding the fact that it is
precisely in heaven that the will attains its most perfect freedom:
it is because God will then be: *et vita, et salus, et victus, et copia, et
gloria, et honor, et pax et omnia bona.*
[344] Here it is quite impossible to imitate: *non peccare posse* ("to
be able not to sin") — *peccare non posse* ("to be unable to sin");
and *posse non mori* ("to be able not to die") — *mori non posse*
("to be unable to die").
[345] Cf. Prov. 8.35 in the Septuagint version.
[346] Rom. 6.23.
[347] *Stipendium* (Augustine takes up the word used in the text he
has just quoted from St. Paul) is the "pay" received for military
service. In a transferred sense the word can also designate such
service itself: *stipendia merere* = "to perform military service."
[348] Cf. John 1.18.
[349] Rom. 9.21.
[350] Cf. Jer. 9.23 f.; 1 Cor. 1.31; 2 Cor. 10.16-18.
[351] 1 Tim. 2.5.
[352] Cf. *Serm.* 174.2: *Si homo non periisset, Filius hominis non*

venisset. Augustine always maintained that the Word became flesh because of sin.

[353] This entire passage and others like it have at times been understood to teach the *absolute* necessity of the God-Man in order to bring about our reconciliation with God. See, for example, A. Sabatier, *The Doctrine of the Atonement and its Historical Evolution* (trans. by V. Leuliette, London 1904) 52. However, St. Augustine made it clear in many other passages that the Incarnation of the Word was necessary only because God Himself had freely willed it. See *De Trin.* 13. 10. 13; *De agone Christ.* 11. 12.

[354] A. Harnack, *op. ˊ*   5. 205 says: " This expression *homo-Deus* was not used,·so far as I know, before Augustine."

[355] *De tanto Mediatoris sacramento* — a most befitting title for the recapitulation which St. Augustine has just given of his teaching on the God-Man! As remarked by C. Mohrmann (*op. cit.* 126 f.), it is surprising that the term *mediator* had not found a place in the vocabulary of the legal-minded Romans long before the advent of Christianity. The word seems to occur first in the so-called Itala version of the Bible. As we have it, it is a loan word from the Greek μεσίτης (cf. Gal. 3. 19; 1 Tim. 2. 5; Heb. 8. 6, 9. 15, 12. 24). Cf. F. Prat, *op. cit.* 2. 115-17; 199-200. Hilary of Poitiers is the first Latin writer to employ the term often. After him Augustine uses it constantly—ten times in our *Enchiridion* and approximately fifty times in the *De civitate Dei.*

[356] For the history of this idea in patristic literature, see J. Quasten, "Die Grabinschrift des Beratius Nikatoras," *Mitteil. d. Deutsch. Arch. Inst.-Röm. Abt.* 53 (1938) 50-69.

[357] Recall the immortal pages of the *Confessions* 9. 12 f., in which St. Augustine begs his friends to offer prayers and the Holy Sacrifice of the Mass for the repose of the soul of his mother. — The Mass for the dead was well known in Africa from the earliest times. See Tertullian, *De corona* 3. Cf. F. J. Dölger, ΙΧΘΥΣ 2 (Münster 1922) 564; A. C. Rush, *Death and Burial in Christian Antiquity* (Stud. in Christ. Ant. 1, Washington 1941) 74 f. Bishop Evodius, writing to St. Augustine about the death of a pious youth, says that they offered the sacrifice of the Eucharist for him on the third day after his death (cf. Augustine, *Ep.* 158. 2). See also E. Freistedt, *Altchristliche Totengedächtnistage und ihre Beziehung zum Jenseitsglauben und Totenkultus der Antike* (Münster 1928) 35 f.

[358] St. Augustine preached the giving of alms to the poor as a

means of relieving the souls of the dead. Cf. especially his *Ep.* 22. 6. See J. Quasten, "Vetus Superstitio et Nova Religio: The Problem of Refrigerium in the Ancient Church of North Africa," *Harv. Theol. Rev.* 33 (1940) 262 f.

[359] Even today, apart from the Scriptures there is no better argument than this one for the existence of purgatory, an intermediate though temporary state between heaven and hell.

[360] Ista quae pro defunctis commendandis frequentat Ecclesia.

[361] 2 Cor. 5. 10; cf. Rom. 14. 10-12.

[362] Although a great manifestation of God's loving mercy, purgatory nevertheless presents an aspect full of tragedy. For, while suffering accepted in this life out of love for God can increase for all eternity our capacity for heavenly joy, the sufferings of purgatory, no matter how long or how God-lovingly they are endured, will never increase the soul's merits for heaven.

[363] Aut . . . ut sit plena remissio, aut certe ut tolerabilior fiat ipsa damnatio.

[364] The idea of the two cities, the *civitas Dei* and the *civitas diaboli*, is a favorite one of St. Augustine. He makes use of it in *De cat. rud.* 31, 37 (cf. J. P. Christopher, ACW 2. 61, 67); *De vera rel.* 50; *Enarr. in Ps.* 61. 6, 64. 2; etc. He developed it fully in his *De civitate Dei*. It seems that Augustine borrowed this idea from Tyconius the Donatist, who had brought it out in strong relief in his *Commentary on the Apocalypse*, composed shortly before 350.

[365] Ps. 76. 10.

[366] Rom. 9. 23.

[367] Note the paronomasia: sed de Deo *miserante* de *miseria* liberantur.

[368] Matt. 25. 46.

[369] *Ibid.*

[370] In earlier works St. Augustine had shown a far more uncompromising attitude toward speculation concerning periodic interruptions of the torments of hell; cf. his *In Ioan. Ev. tractatus* (98. 8), written 416-17, and the *Enarr. in Ps.* 105. 2, written probably at about the same time. The fact that by the year 421, when he composed the *Enchiridion*, he appears to have adopted a more tolerant view of the theory (cf. also *De civ. Dei* 21. 24), may be bound up with the appearance in the West of the *Apocalypse of Paul*. In this apocryphal work Christ grants the damned a respite from their torments on every Sunday, the day on which He rose from the dead. Cf. M. R. James, *The Apocryphal New Testament*

(Oxford 1924) 548 f. The Spanish poet Prudentius gave the theory a place in his verse (*Cath.* 5. 125 ff.). It also found its way into the Mozarabic liturgy. For further details, read the interesting study by S. Merkle, "Augustin über eine Unterbrechung der Höllen-strafen," *Aurelius Augustinus: Die Festschrift der Görres-Gesell-schaft zum 1500. Todestage des heiligen Augustinus* (Cologne 1930) 197-202; L. G. A. Getino, *Del gran numero de los que se salvan y de la mitigacion de las penas eternas* (Madrid 1934).

[371] Cf. Ps. 30. 20.

[372] Cf. A. Lehaut, *L'éternité des peines de l'enfer dans S. Augustin* (Paris 1912).

[373] See H. Doms, "Ewige Verklärung und ewige Verwerfung nach dem hl. Augustinus," *Divus Thomas* 10 (1932) 275 ff.

[374] Cf. 1 Cor. 3. 1 ff.; also *Conf.* 7. 10. 17.

[375] Jer. 17. 5.

[376] Matt. 6. 9 f.

[377] *Ibid.* 6. 11-13.—In this part of the Lord's Prayer St. Augustine has two striking variant readings. St. Jerome had replaced the older reading *panem nostrum cottidianum* ("our daily bread") with *panem nostrum supersubstantialem* ("our supersubstantial bread"). Although since approximately the year 400 St. Augustine generally followed the Vulgate for the Gospels, in this instance he adhered to the form "our daily bread" (cf. Luke 11. 3), which, it is interesting to observe, are also the words we use in saying the prayer. The second variant is *ne nos inferas in tentationem* ("bring us not into temptation") for *ne nos inducas in tentationem* ("lead us not into temptation"), which is St. Jerome's wording. St. Cyprian used the form *ne patiaris nos induci in tentationem* ("do not suffer us to be led into temptation"). From the year 393 until his death St. Augus-tine never deviated from his version, though he was familiar with the others. Cf. D. De Bruyne, "Saint Augustin reviseur de la Bible," *Misc. Agost.* 2 (Rome 1931) 595-99. St. Ambrose's form (*De sacr.* 5. 4. 20) is almost identical with St. Cyprian's: *ne patiaris induci nos in tentationem.* Concerning this form St. Augustine states (*De serm. in monte* 2. 9. 30) that it is an explanatory version of *ne nos inducas in tentationem.* Cf. F. H. Chase, *The Lord's Prayer in the Early Church* (Texts and Studies 1. 3, Cambridge 1891) 71-167; J. Moffatt, "Augustine on the Lord's Prayer," *Expositor* 18 (1919) 259-72.

[378] Cf. Luke 11. 2-4.

[379] Cf. 1 Cor. 13. 13.

[380] See G. Combès, *La charité d'après* S. *Augustin* (Paris 1934).

[381] Gal. 5. 6.

[382] Cf. Matt. 7. 7; Luke 11. 9-13; John 16. 23 f.

[383] Fides namque *impetrat* quod lex *imperat*. For the "Gift of God," mentioned in the following, see above, n. 120.

[384] For the four states of man which St. Augustine distinguishes, see R. Jolivet, "La doctrine augustinienne de l'illumination," *Rev. de philos.* 30 (1930) 382-502; the same, *Dieu soleil des esprits* (Paris 1934); H. D. Simonin, "La conversion chez Plotin et S. Augustin," *La vie spirit.* 42 (1935) 54-62. Elsewhere Augustine divides all history into six epochs (*aetates*); cf. the passages (e. g., *De cat. rud.* 22. 39, *De civ. Dei* 22. 30) collected by J. P. Christopher, ACW 2 (1946) 136 nn. 249 and 250.

[385] Rom. 3. 20.

[386] 2 Peter 2. 19.

[387] Cf. Rom. 7. 7.

[388] Here the word *praevaricatio* is used. This and *transgressio* are terms of old standing (Tertullian, Cyprian) for "original sin" (Rom. 5. 14: *praevaricatio Adae*). Cf. G. Koffmane, *Geschichte des Kirchenlateins* (Breslau 1879) 69. When the priest vests for Mass and puts on the stole, he says this ancient prayer: Redde mihi, Domine, stolam immortalitatis quam perdidi in *praevaricatione primi parentis.* . . .

[389] Rom. 5. 20.

[390] Cf. Rom. 8. 14.

[391] Cf. Gal. 5. 17.

[392] Cf. Rom. 1. 17; Hab. 2. 4; Gal. 3. 11; Heb. 10. 38.

[393] Wisd. 11. 21

[394] John 3. 8.

[395] Consult Augustine, *De pecc. mer. et remiss.* 2. 28. 46: Si continuo (post baptismum) consequatur ab hac vita emigratio, non erit omnino, quod obnoxium hominem teneat, solutis omnibus, quae tenebant. See V. Cuttaz, *Les effets du baptême* (Juvisy-sur-Orge 1934).

[396] Rom. 14. 9.

[397] Ps. 87. 6.

[398] 1 Tim. 1. 5.

[399] Cf. Rom. 5. 5.

[400] Matt. 22. 40.

[401] 1 Tim. 1. 5 and 1 John 4. 16.

[402] Matt. 5. 27.

[403] 1 Cor. 7. 1.

[404] Cf. H. Arendt, *Der Liebesbegriff bei Augustin* (Berlin 1929).

[405] Cf. 2 Cor. 5. 7; also 1 Cor. 13. 12.

[406] 1 Cor. 4. 5.

[407] John 15. 13.—In this treatise St. Augustine has drawn incessantly upon the treasury of Sacred Scripture. His great familiarity with the Bible has ever astonished his readers. Since the sixteenth century various attempts have been made to reconstruct parts of Augustine's Bible from his Scriptural quotations, or to list and count such quotations. A collection made by P. de Lagarde and now preserved at the University of Göttingen, contains 42,816 citations, 13,276 taken from the Old Testament, 29,540 from the New. Cf. D. De Bruyne, " Saint Augustin reviseur de la Bible," *Misc. Agost.* 2 (Rome 1931) 522.

INDEX

INDEX